Patriotic
Patterns & Clip Art

Compiled by Dona Herweck and Ina Massler Levin
Illustrated by Blanca Apodaca, Cheryl Buhler, Sue Fullam,
Paula Spence, Keith Vasconcelles, and Theresa Wright

Teacher Created Materials, Inc.
P.O. Box 1214
Huntington Beach, CA 92647
© 1991 Teacher Created Materials, Inc.
Made in U.S.A.
ISBN 1-55734-142-7

The classroom teacher may reproduce copies of materials in this book for classroom use only. The reproduction of any part for an entire school or school system is strictly prohibited. No part of this publication may be transmitted, stored, or recorded in any form without written permission from the publisher.

Table of Contents

Introduction 2
Uses for the Patterns and Clip Art 3
Reproducing the Patterns and Clip Art 4
American History 5
Americana 17
Democracy 36
Landmarks 40
Monuments and Memorials 42
Patriotic Holidays 49
    Columbus Day ♦ *Flag Day* ♦ *Independence Day* ♦ *Martin Luther King, Jr. Day* ♦ *Memorial Day* ♦ *President's Day* ♦ *Veteran's Day*
People 70
Symbols 74

Introduction

Patriotic Patterns and Clip Art is a collection of reproducible art that can be used throughout the year. Patriotic symbols, places, people, and holidays, and so much more fill its 80 pages. And all are organized for quick and easy access into the 8 useful sections.

Best of all the material here will enable teachers to personalize notes, worksheets, and activities so that:

- Lessons and activities spring to life.
- Students are better able to grasp meaning and directions.
- Parents sit up and take notice.

Also found here is a compilation of tips and ideas for reproducing and using the patterns and clip art. From sprucing up a note to clarifying directions to perking up bulletin boards, *Patriotic Patterns and Clip Art* will prove an invaluable aid for every teacher.

Uses for the Patterns and Clip Art

There are many ways to use the patterns and clip art found in this book. Some suggestions are:

- Decorations for lessons, bulletin boards, and banners
- Parent communications
- Invitations, announcements, and awards
- Name tags and place cards
- Clarification for activity directions
- Programs, posters, and publicity
- Charts, graphs, and diagrams
- Game boards and puzzles
- Calendars
- Stationery and borders
- Classroom labeling
- Shape books

In addition to the above, some unique uses for them are:

- *Manipulatives:* Duplicate on to tag or heavy paper, laminate if desired, and cut out. Use for counting, sequencing, organizing, classifying, and numerous other activities.
- *Puppets:* Reproduce on heavy paper, color, and cut out. Affix to craft sticks or paper bags to create puppets.
- *Flannel Boards:* Use the art as flannel board patterns, or copy, color, cut out, and affix the art to a strip of sandpaper (rough side out). The sandpaper will adhere to the flannel.
- *Art Projects:* Use the art to create various art projects. These can include coloring pages, mosaics, painting, free-hand copying, pastel or chalk, collages, and more.
- *Publishing:* Enhance student or teacher text with these ready-made illustrations. Combine or use parts of the art to create unique layout and design.
- *Writing Springboards:* Duplicate and frame or mount; laminate if desired. Use as story starters, descriptive writing, writing for detail, characterizations, and so forth.
- *Centers:* Identify centers and illustrate, define, and explain center activities with the corresponding art.

Reproducing the Patterns and Clip Art

There are many ways to reproduce the patterns and clip art found in this book. Here are some of those ways.

Use a Copy Machine

A. Duplicate* and cut out the desired art. Affix to the project. (If copy machine used has enlargement capabilities, you can adjust the size.)

B. To use only a portion of the art, duplicate it and then cover the undesired part. Do so with correction fluid or correction tape. Cut out and affix to the project.

Trace

A. Use tracing paper or tissue to do by hand any of the methods that can be done on a copy machine.

B. Alternately, use a light board. To create your own, hold the art and tracing paper up to a window on a sunny day or place a shadeless lamp under a glass-topped table.

C. To use a ditto, place the clip art on the ditto master, anchoring it with paper clips. Then, trace the outline using a ball point pen or dull pencil, pressing firmly. The image will appear on the dittoed material.

Enlarge

A. Using an opaque projector, project the pattern onto a large sheet of butcher paper attached to the wall. Adjust the distance of the projector from the wall until the desired size is achieved. Turn off the lights in the room for easier copying. Trace around the projected pattern with a permanent marker.

B. Using an overhead projector and a transparency of the art, follow the steps above.

C. Make a grid of evenly spaced squares over the art. Make a blank grid of the desired enlargement size. Draw lines in the blank squares to match the lines in the original grid. For example, if lines are spaced 1 inch apart on the original, draw lines 2 inches apart on the blank to double the size, 3 inches to triple it, etc. Copy exactly what is in each square. This is best done with a simple image.

* It is suggested that you duplicate the art so that it can be used repeatedly. Of course, if desired, simply cut out the art from the book and use. Before doing this, remember that the reverse of the page has art you may wish to keep.

American History

© 1991 Teacher Created Materials, Inc. #142 Patriotic Patterns & Clip Art

American History

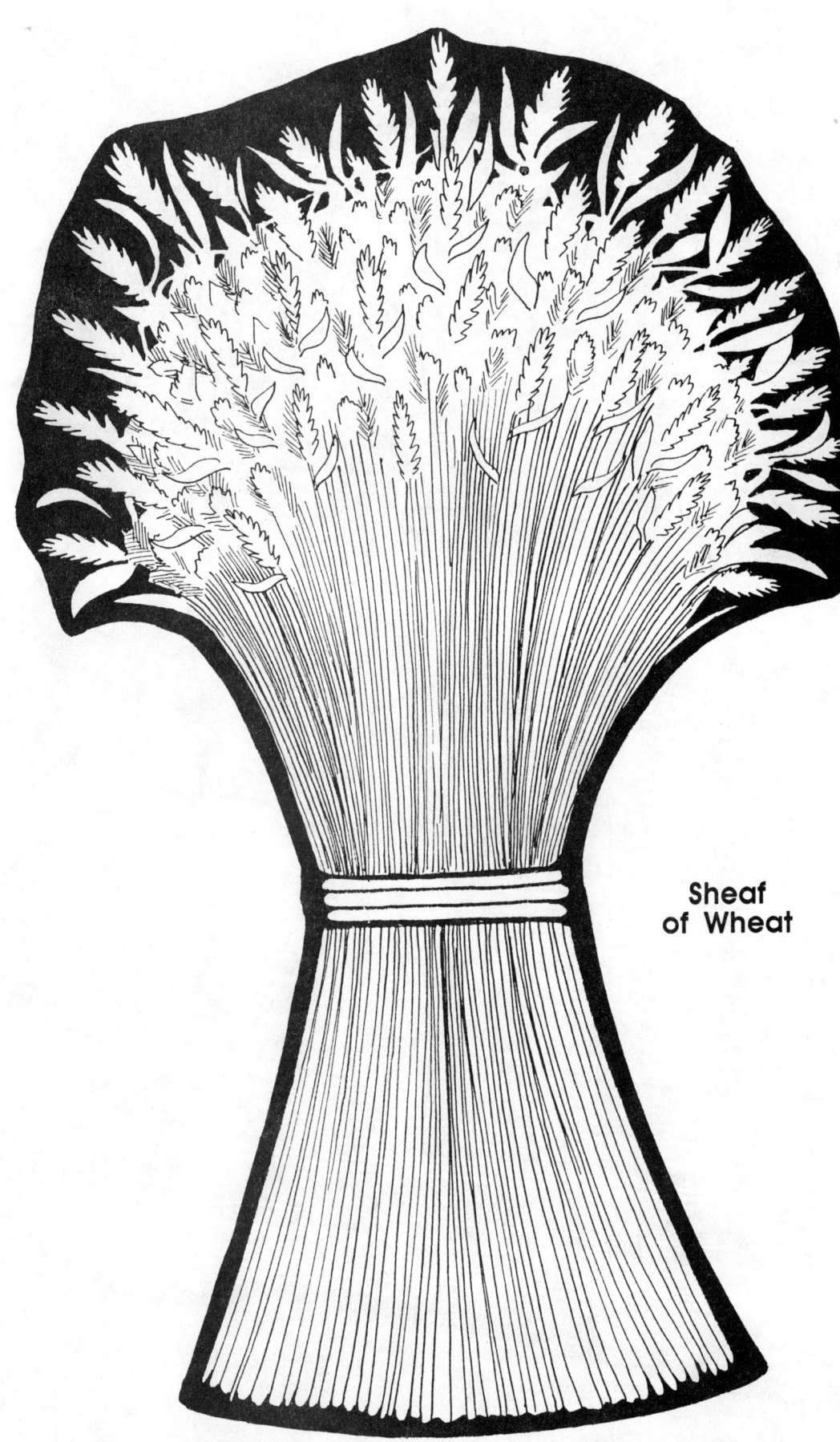

Sheaf of Wheat

American History

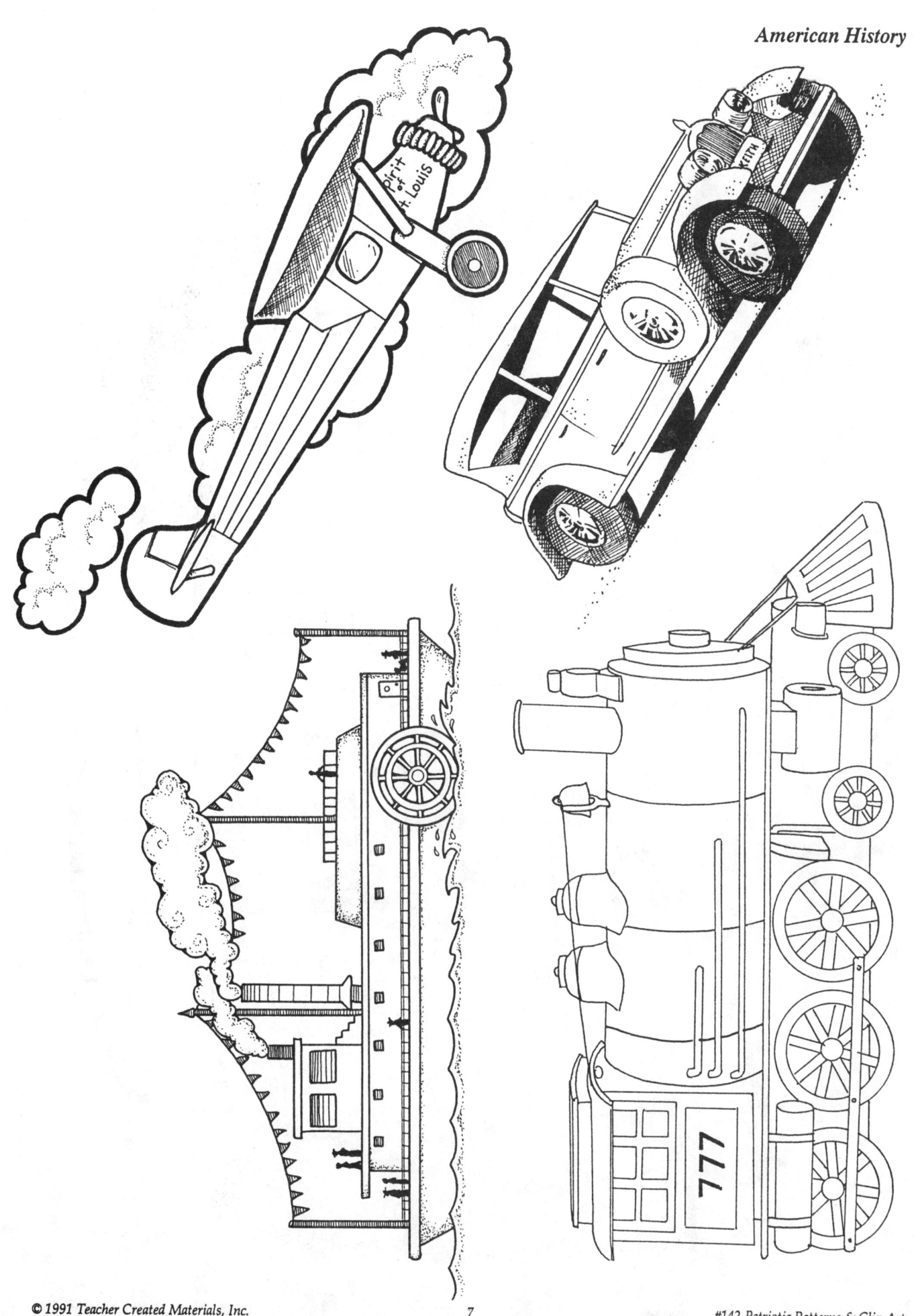

© 1991 Teacher Created Materials, Inc.

#142 Patriotic Patterns & Clip Art

American History

Bushel of Corn

#142 Patriotic Patterns & Clip Art © 1991 Teacher Created Materials, Inc.

American History

Cotton Boll

American History

#142 Patriotic Patterns & Clip Art   10   © 1991 Teacher Created Materials, Inc.

American History

American History

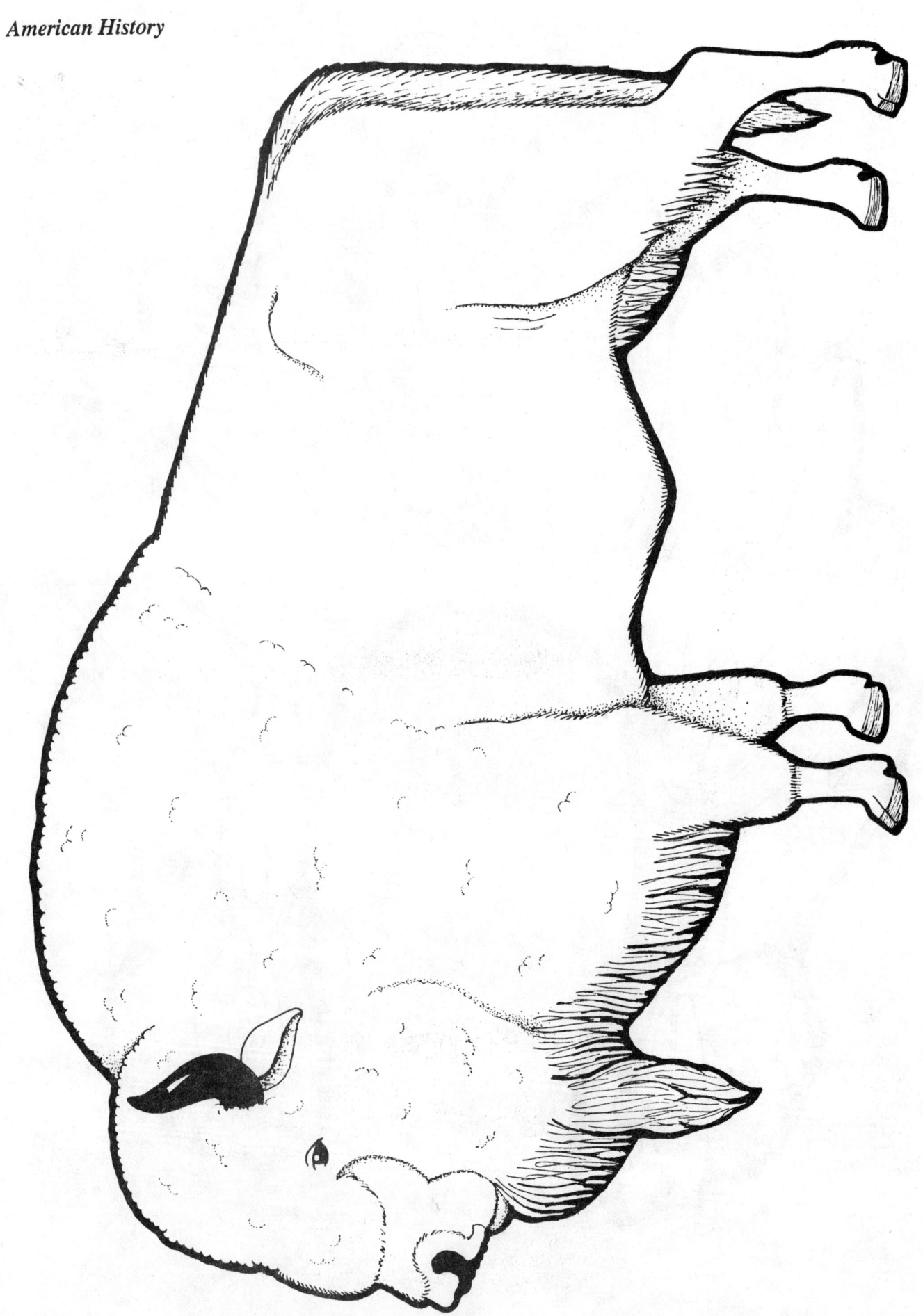

#142 Patriotic Patterns & Clip Art © 1991 Teacher Created Materials, Inc.

American History

The Alamo

Gettysburg

Washington Crossing the Delaware

© 1991 Teacher Created Materials, Inc. #142 Patriotic Patterns & Clip Art

American History

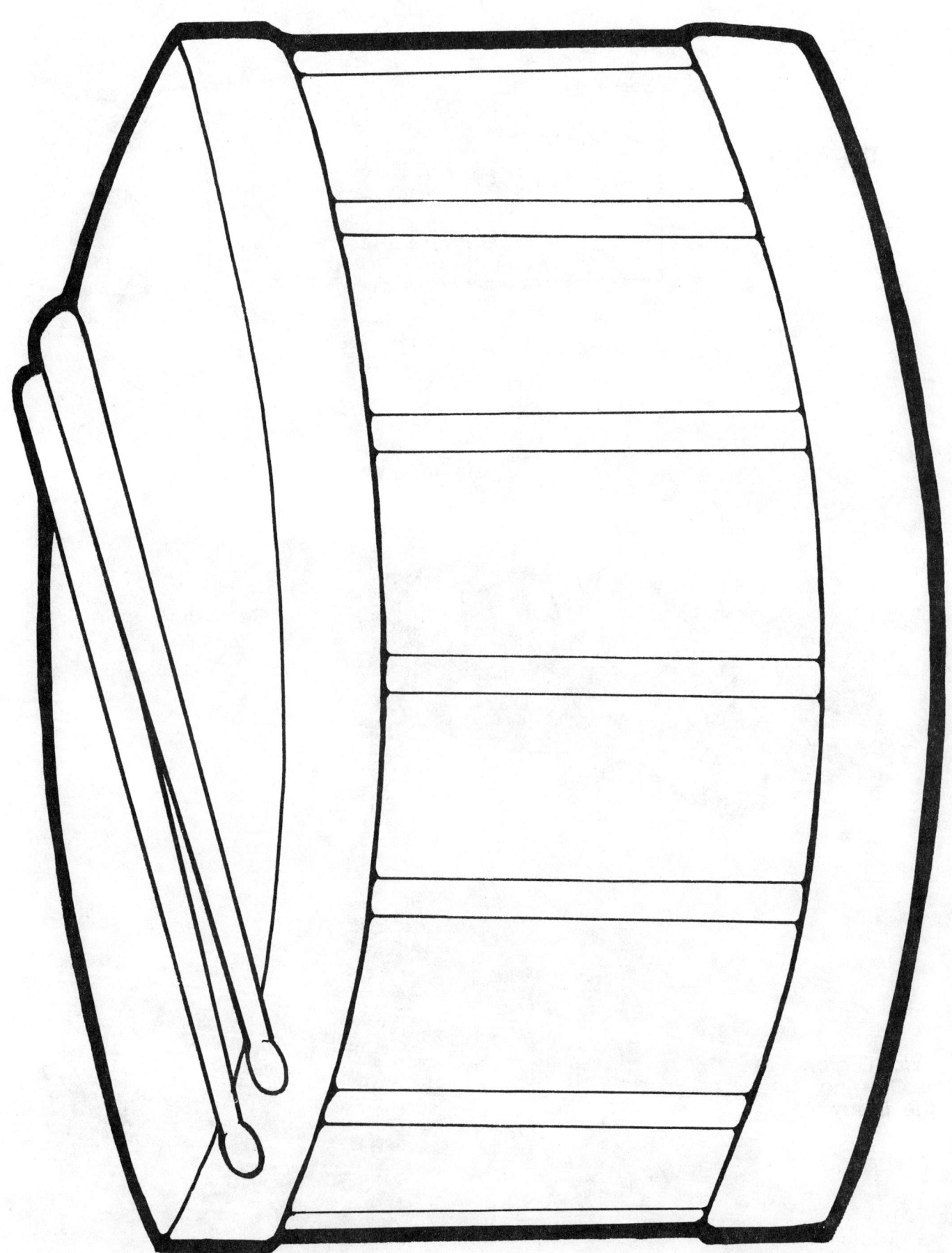

American History

Civil War

Americana

Americana

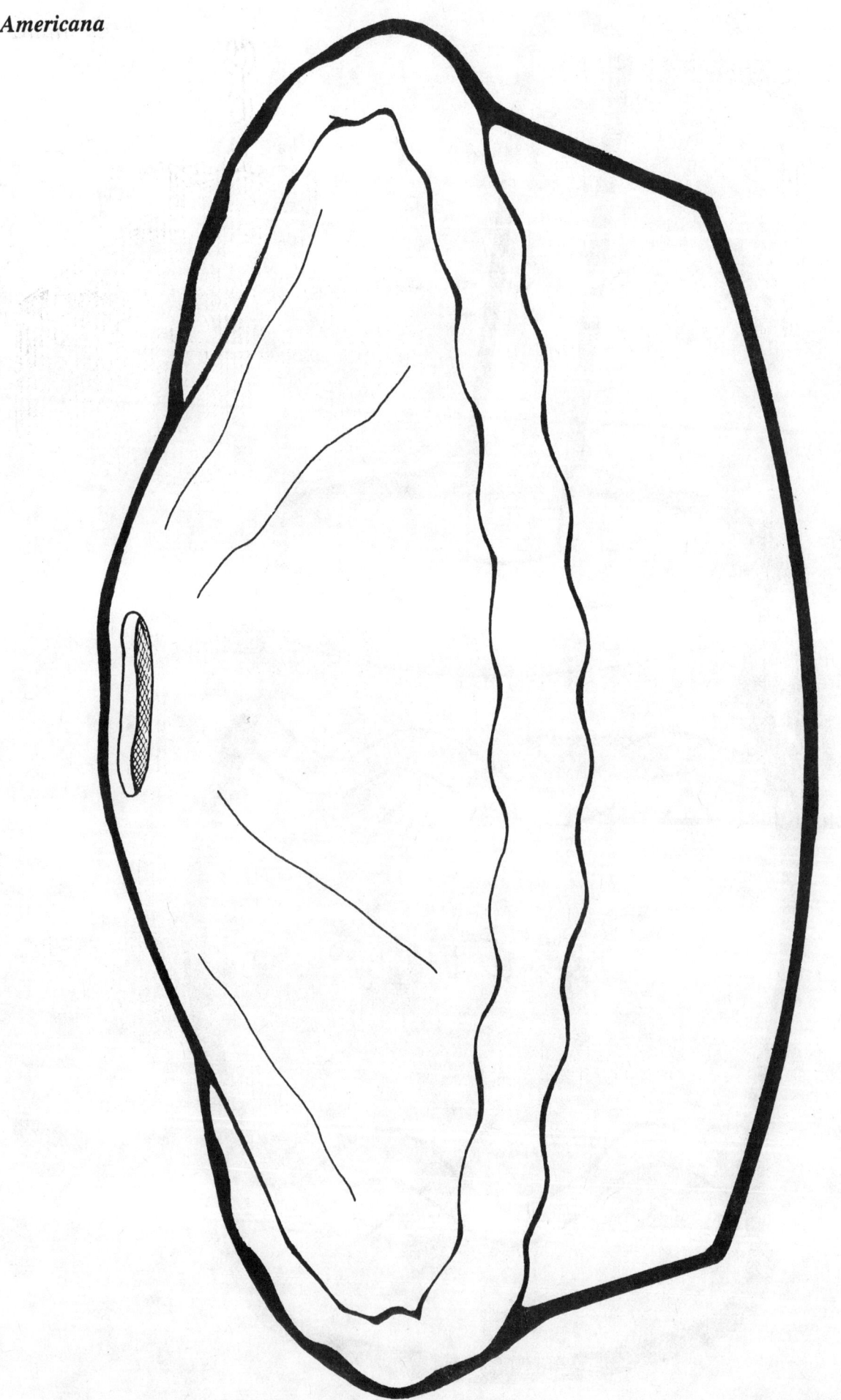

#142 Patriotic Patterns & Clip Art © 1991 Teacher Created Materials, Inc.

Americana

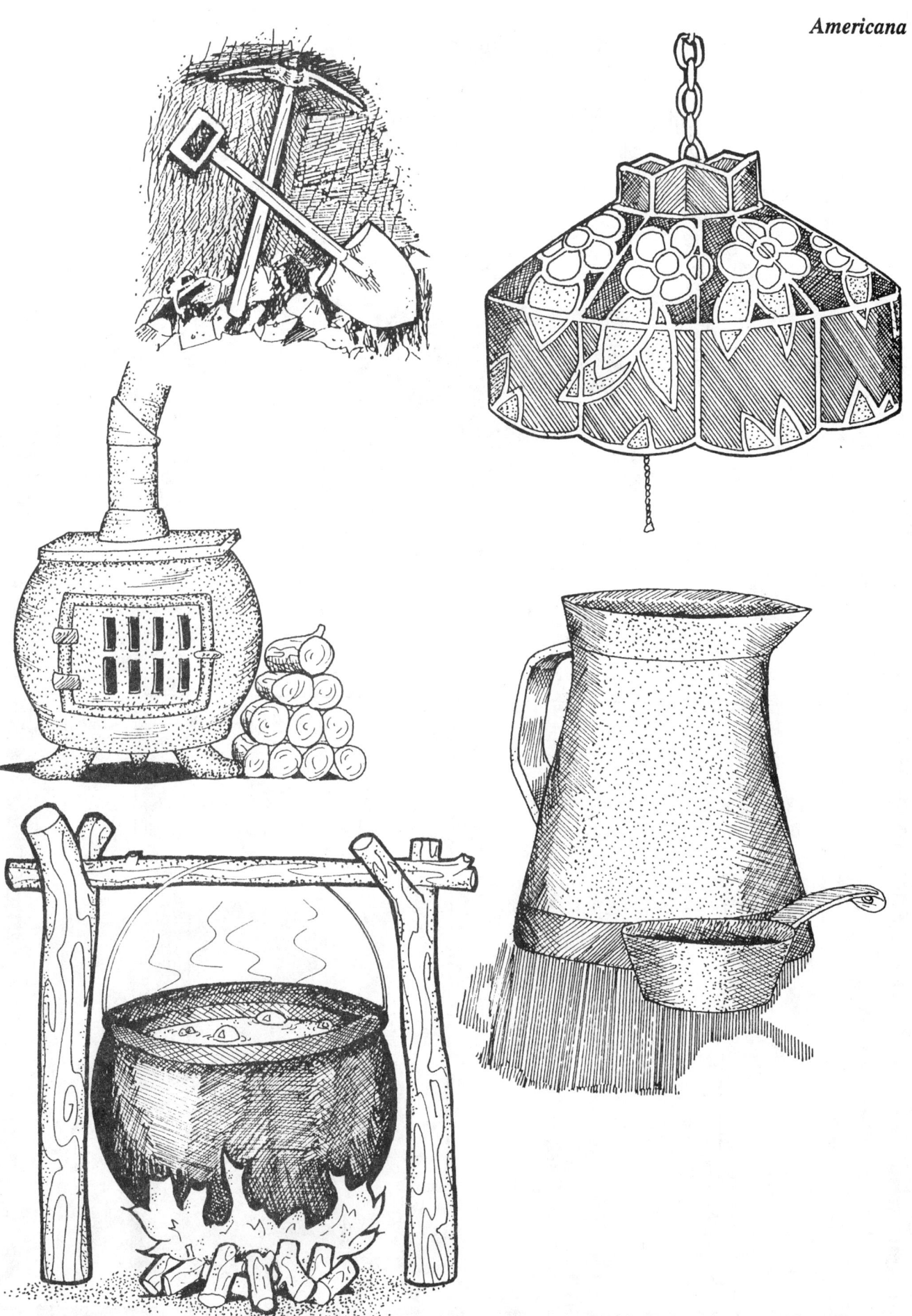

© 1991 Teacher Created Materials, Inc.   #142 Patriotic Patterns & Clip Art

Americana

#142 Patriotic Patterns & Clip Art © 1991 Teacher Created Materials, Inc.

Americana

Americana

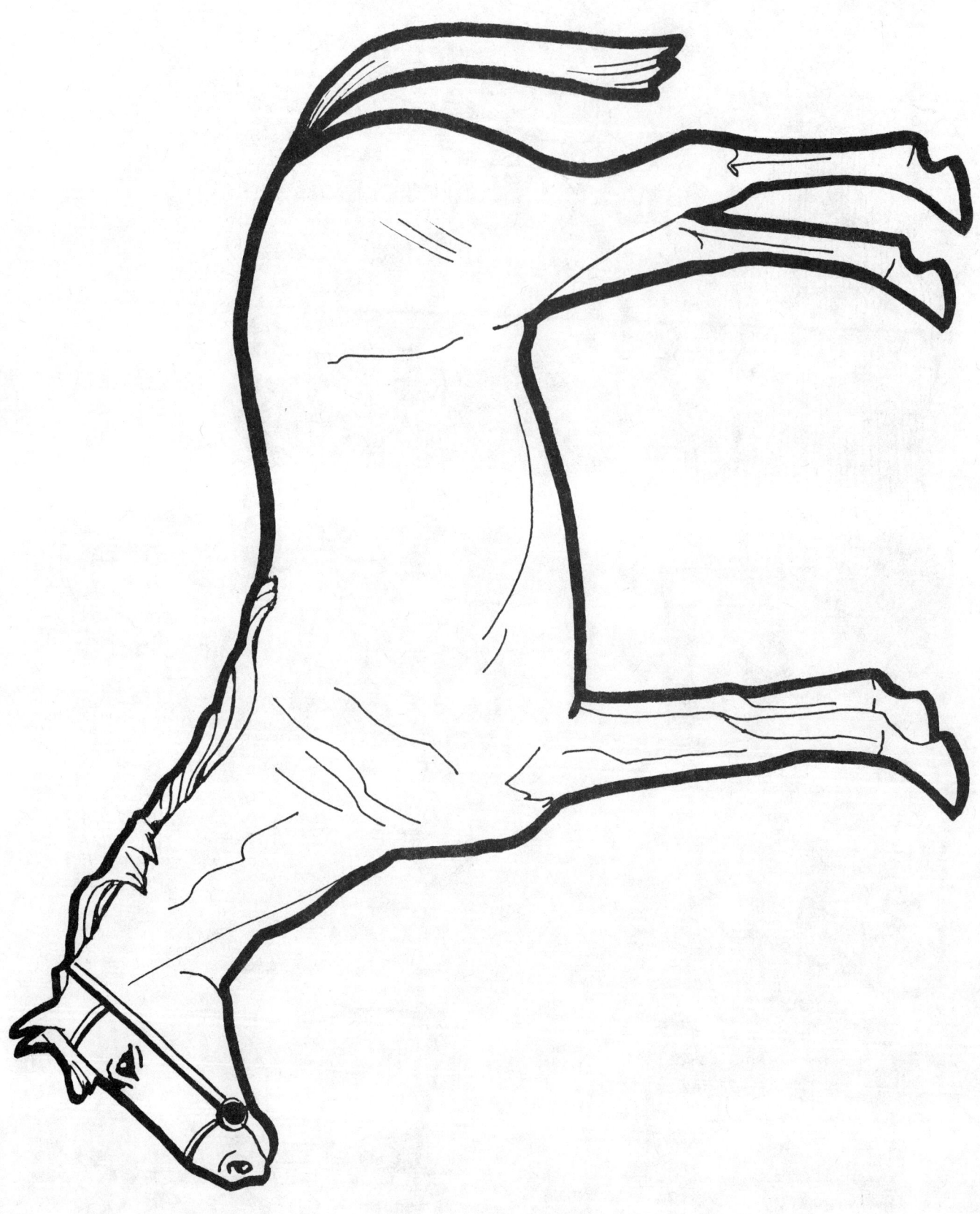

Americana

© 1991 Teacher Created Materials, Inc. #142 Patriotic Patterns & Clip Art

Americana

#142 Patriotic Patterns & Clip Art 24 © 1991 Teacher Created Materials, Inc.

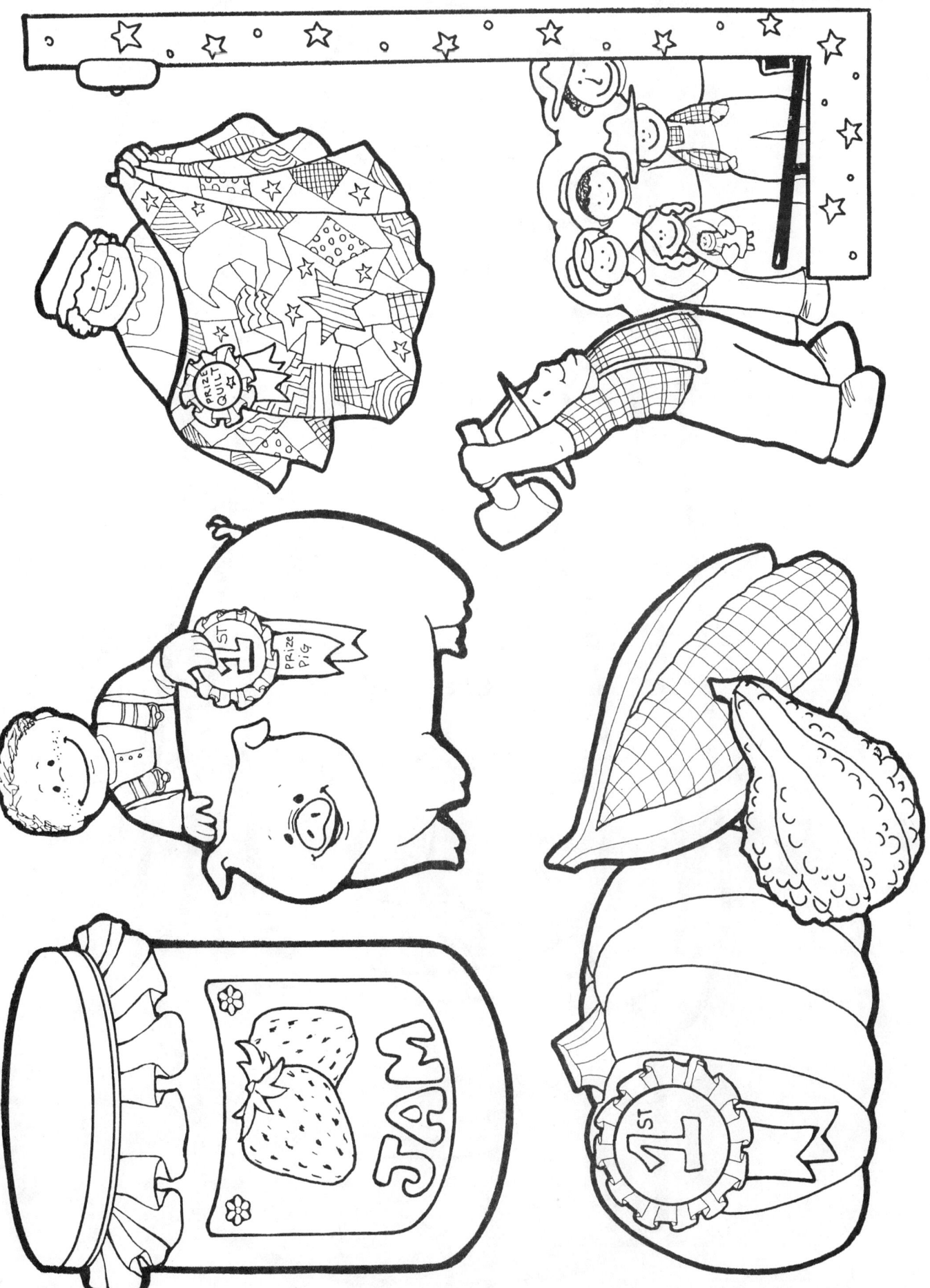

Americana

© 1991 Teacher Created Materials, Inc. 25 #142 Patriotic Patterns & Clip Art

Americana

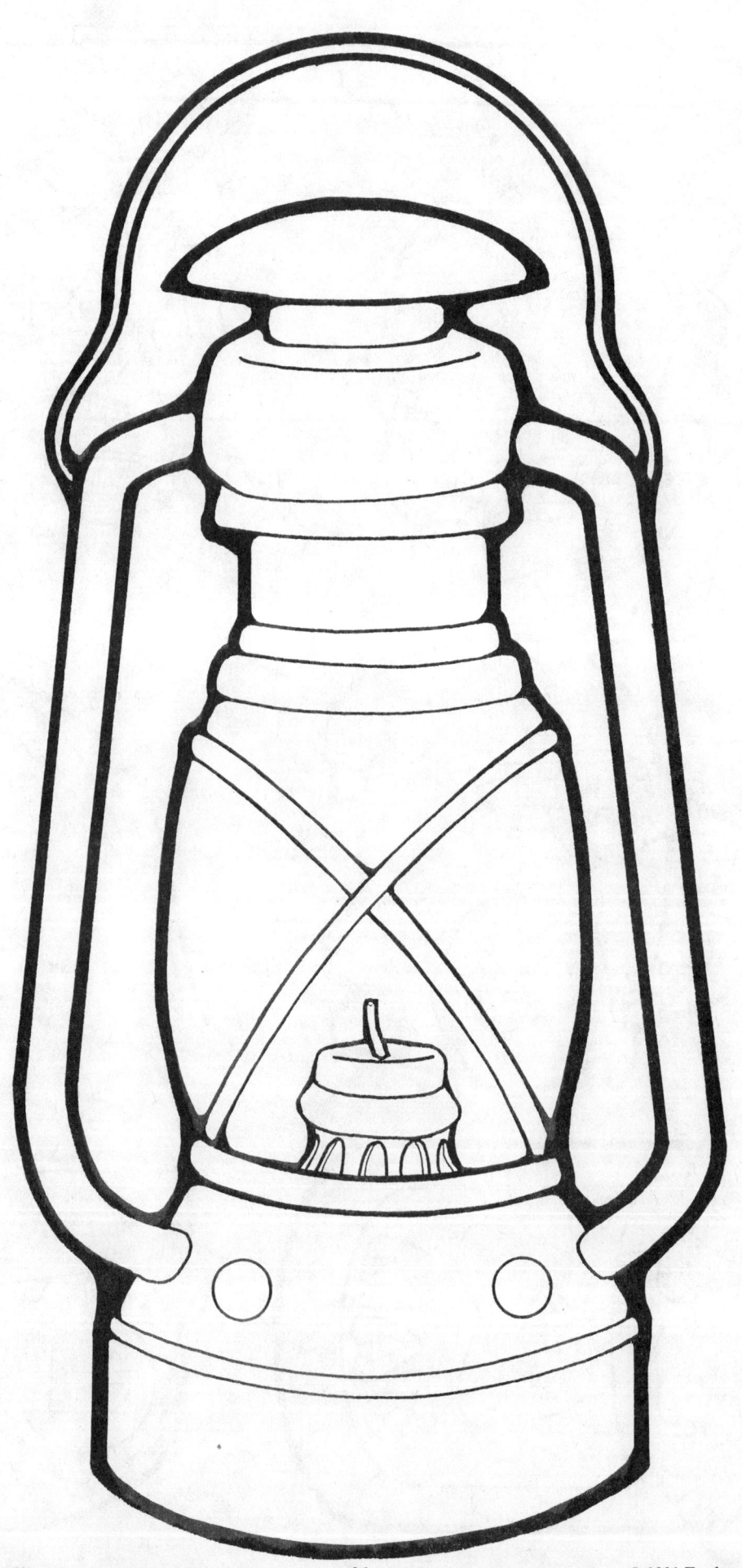

#142 Patriotic Patterns & Clip Art   26   © 1991 Teacher Created Materials, Inc.

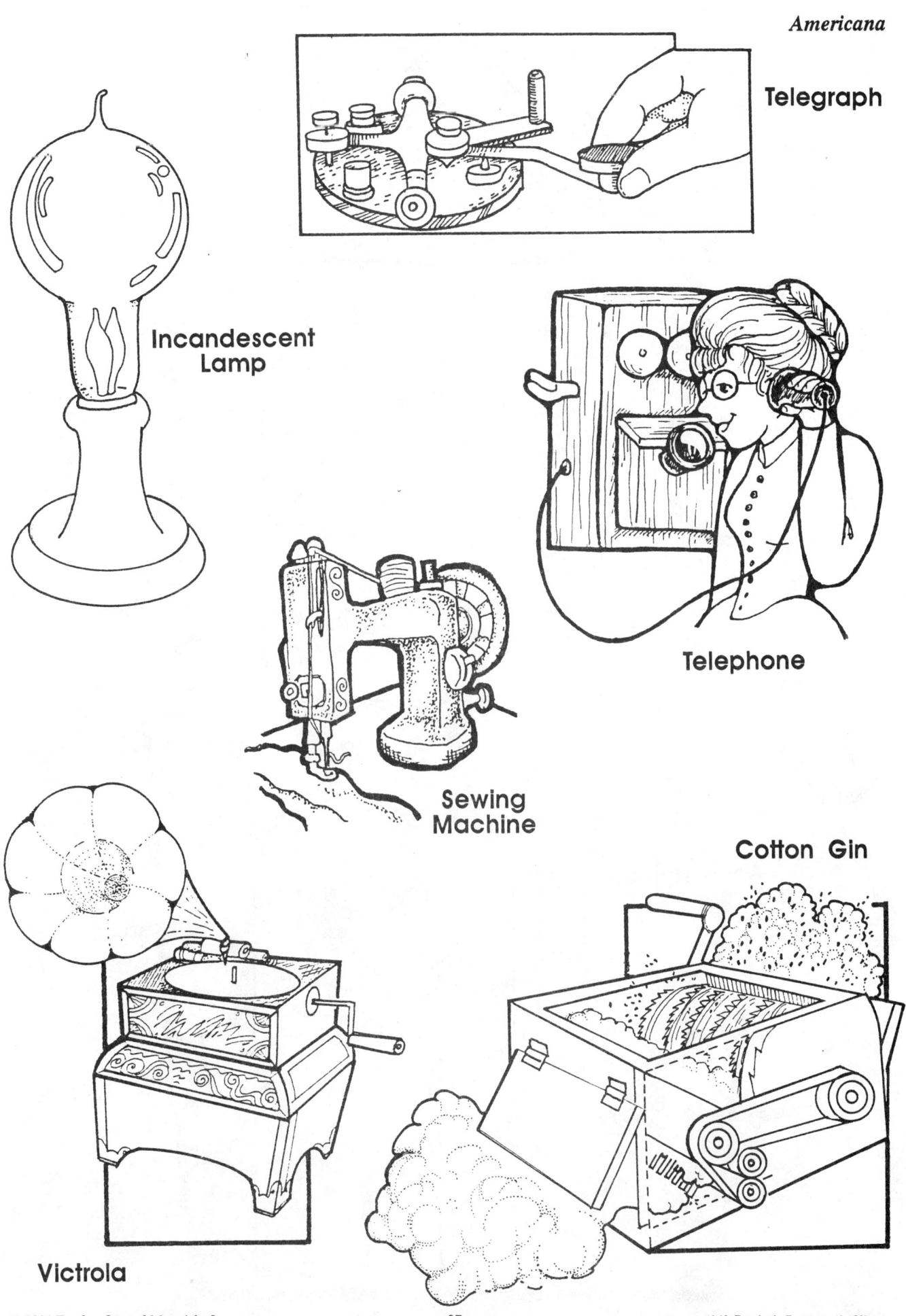

Americana

#142 Patriotic Patterns & Clip Art　　　28　　　© 1991 Teacher Created Materials, Inc.

Americana

Americana

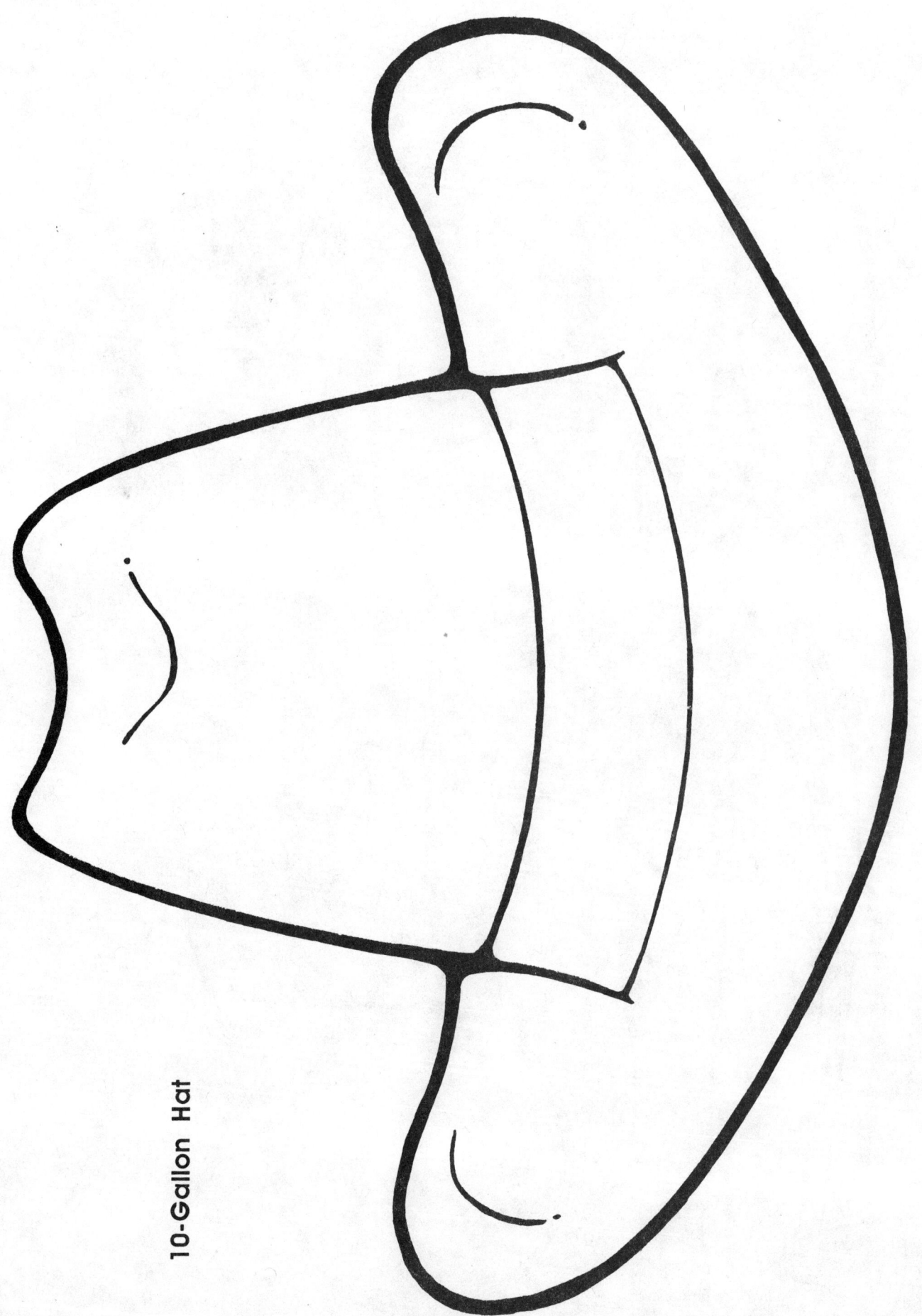

10-Gallon Hat

Americana

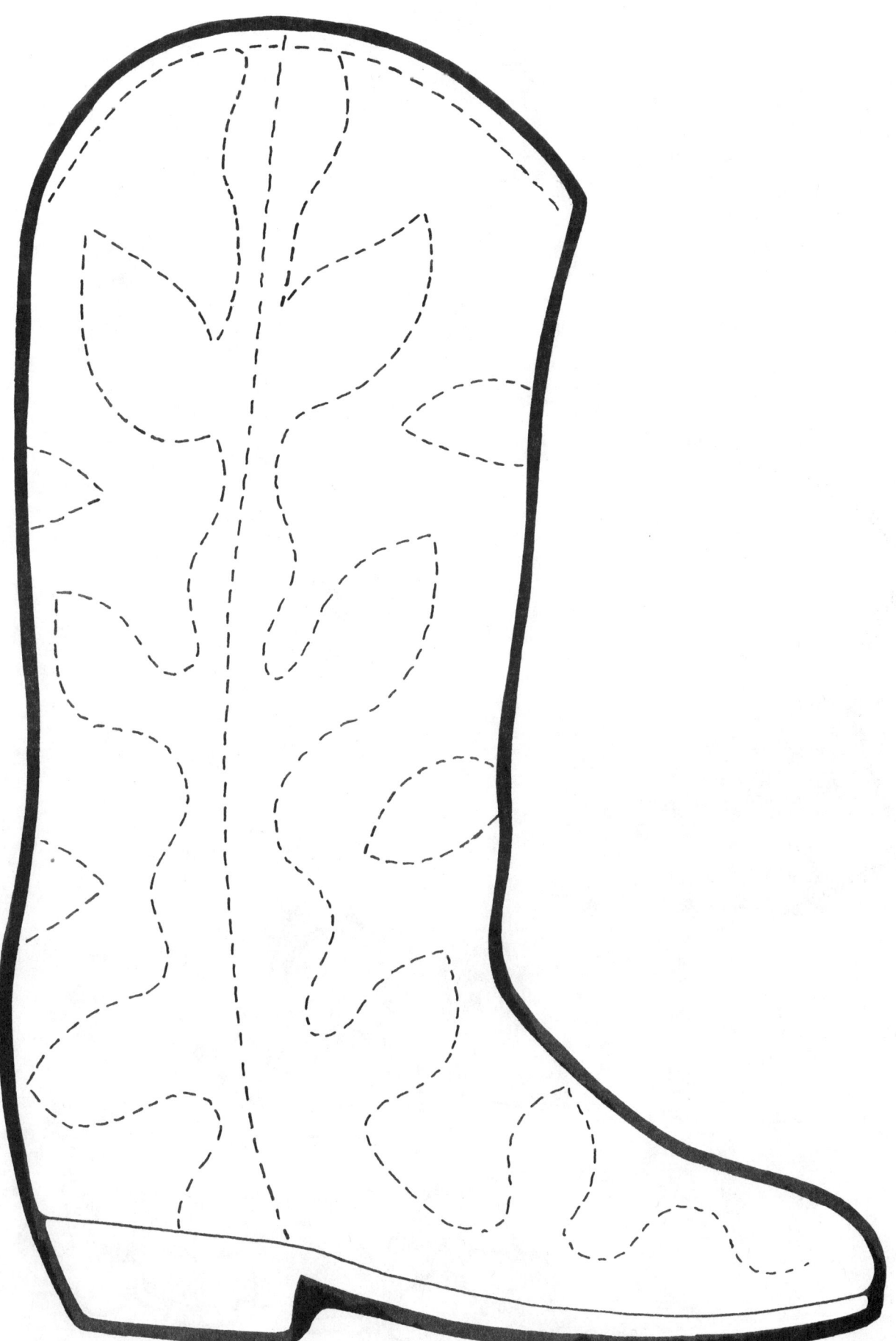

© 1991 Teacher Created Materials, Inc. #142 Patriotic Patterns & Clip Art

Americana

#142 Patriotic Patterns & Clip Art

Americana

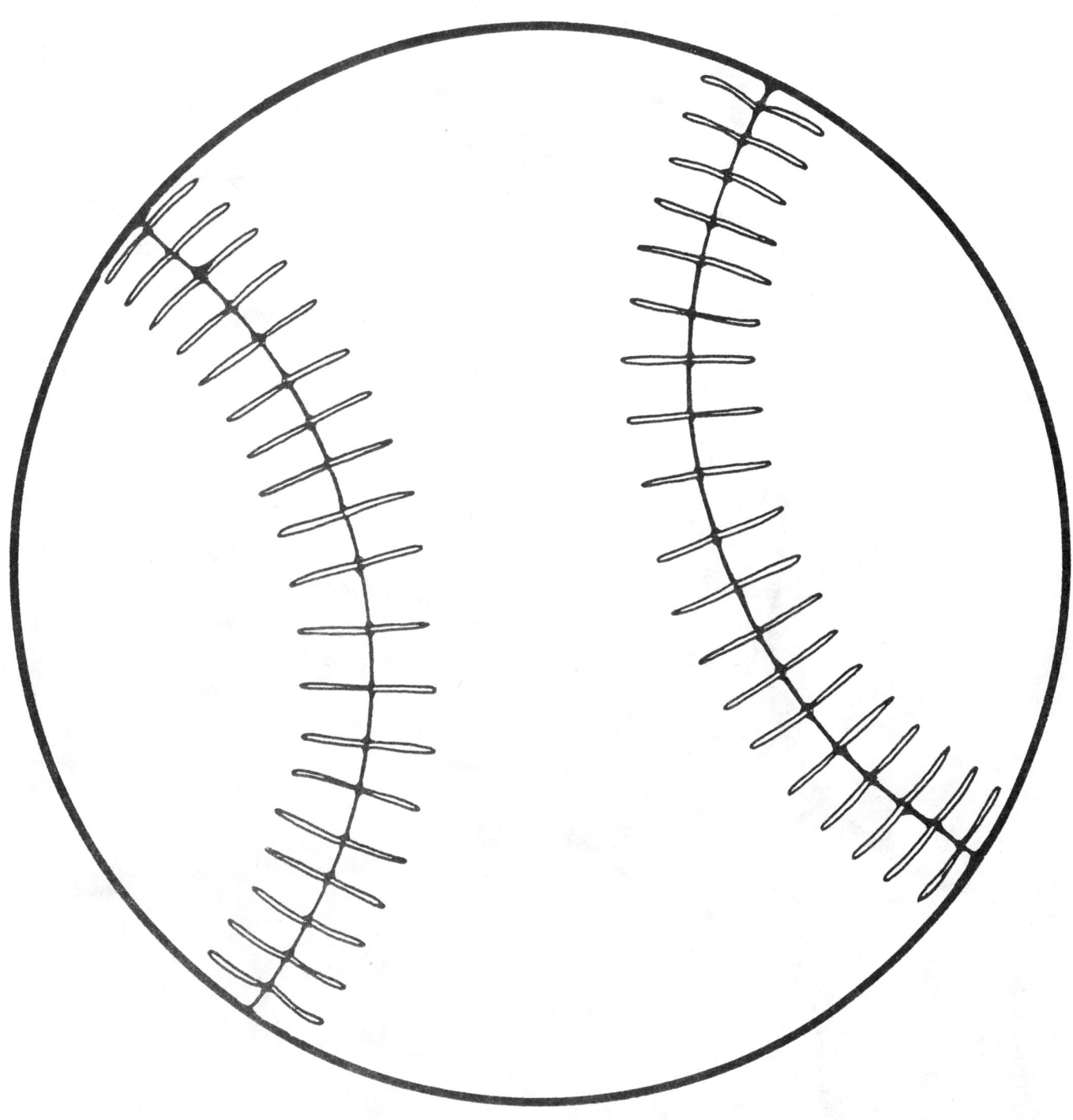

Americana

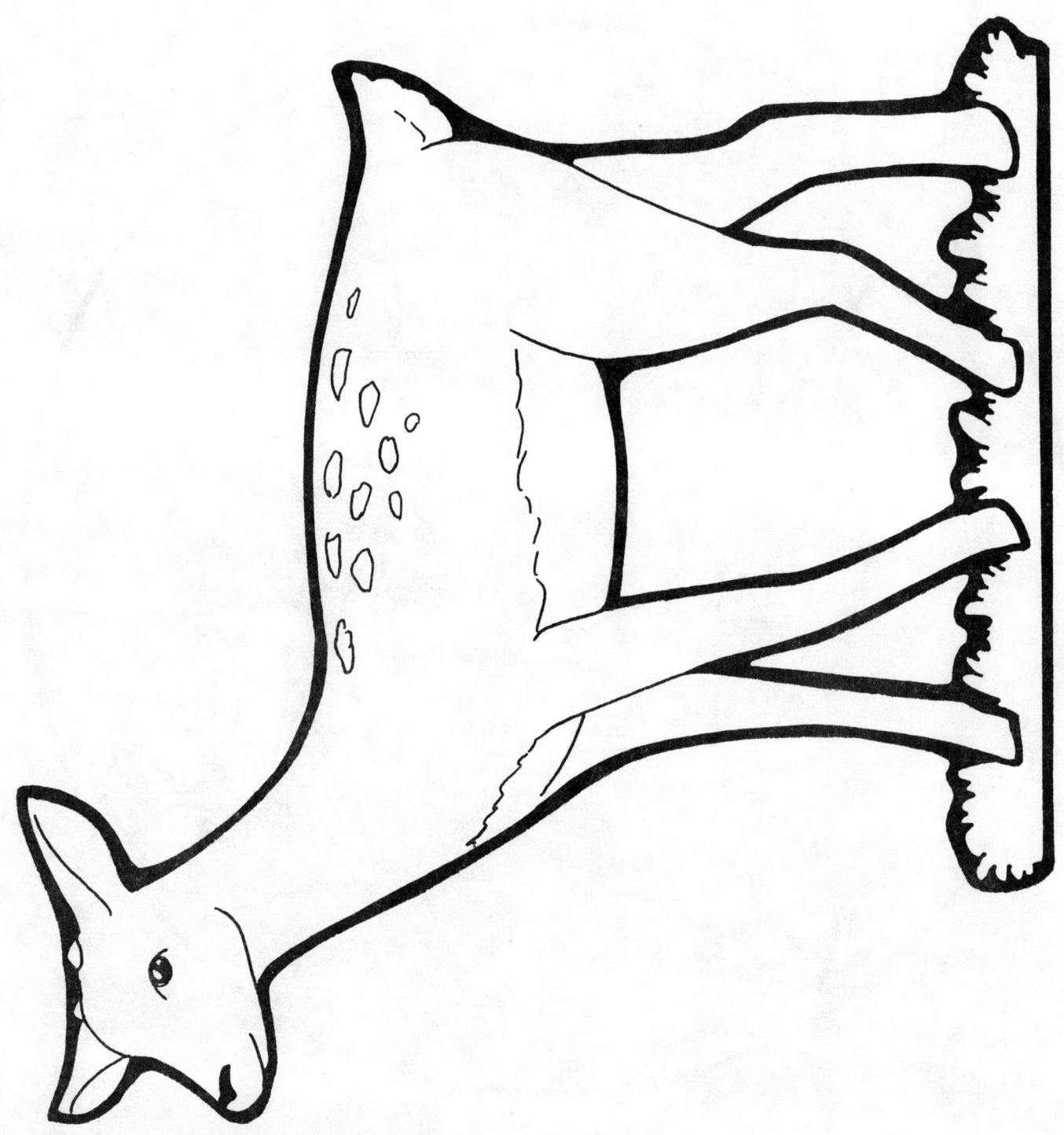

#142 Patriotic Patterns & Clip Art 34 © 1991 Teacher Created Materials, Inc.

Americana

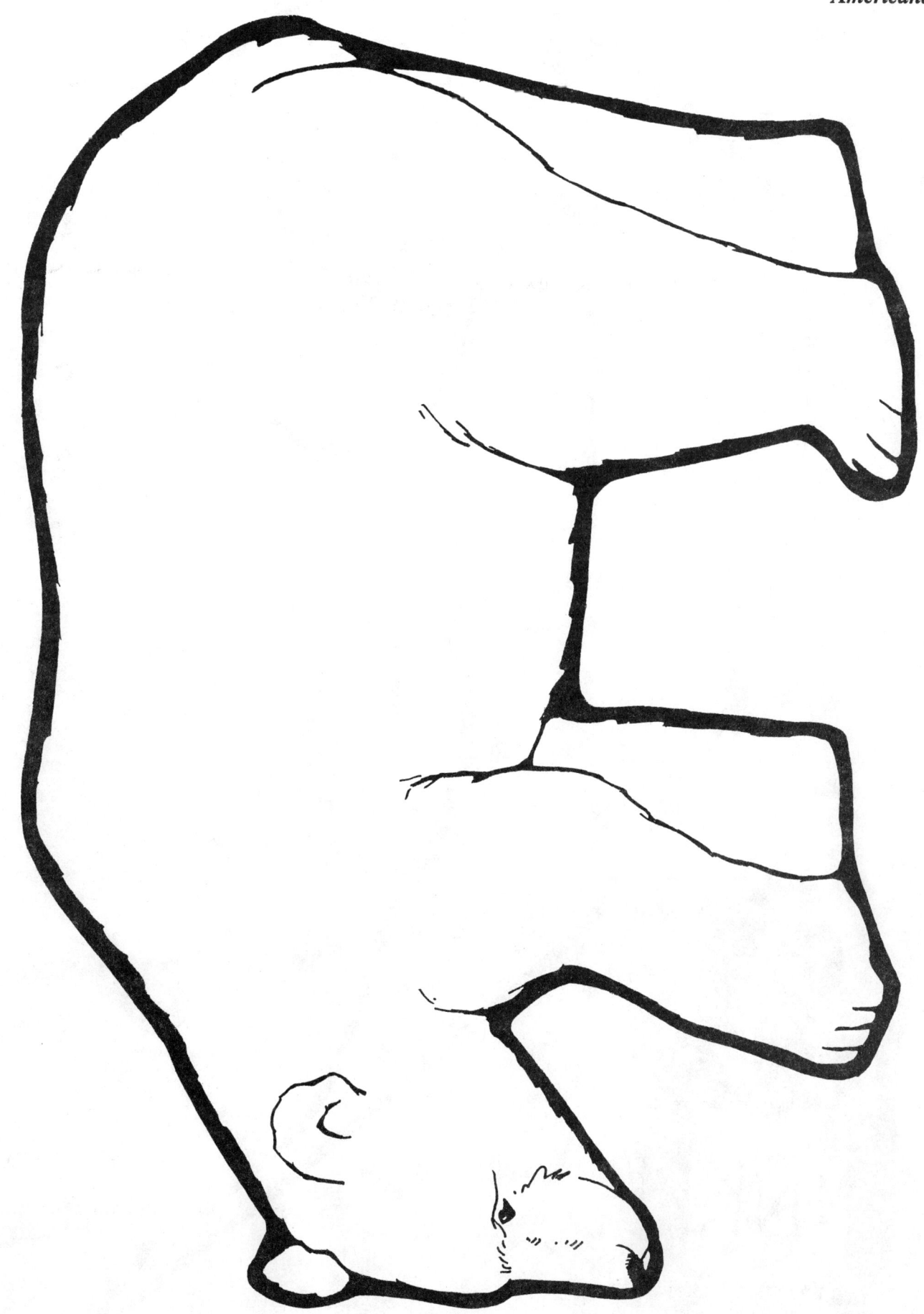

© 1991 Teacher Created Materials, Inc. #142 Patriotic Patterns & Clip Art

Democracy

Democracy

Democracy

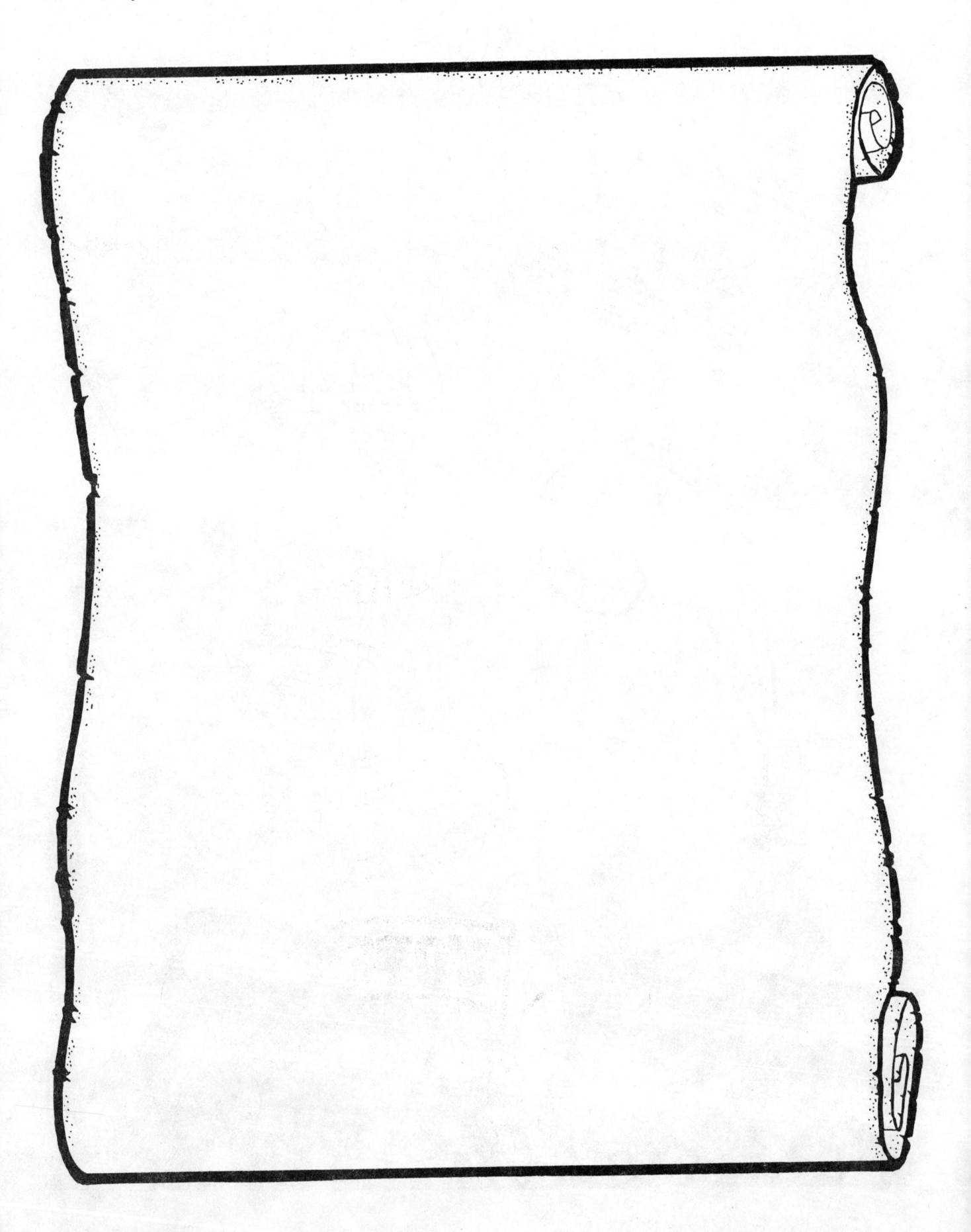

Democracy

Landmarks

Mt. Rainier

Space Needle

Mt. Hood

St. Louis Arch

Old Faithful

Crater Lake

#142 Patriotic Patterns & Clip Art   40   © 1991 Teacher Created Materials, Inc.

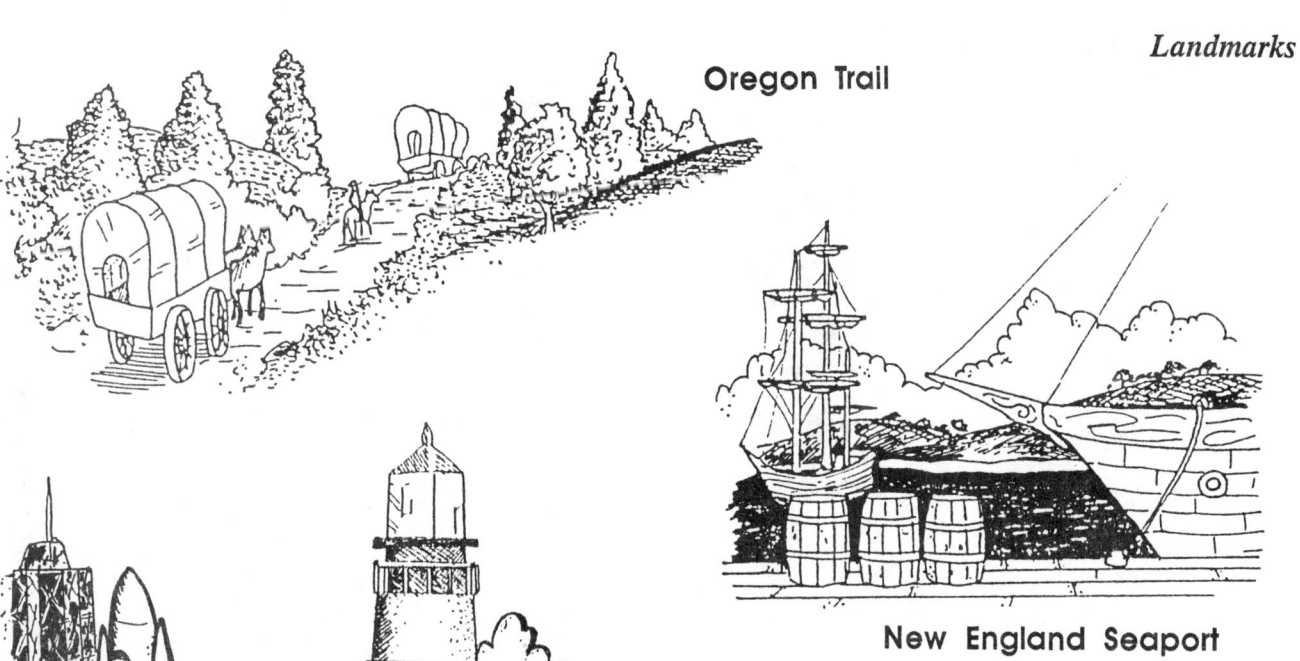

Landmarks

Oregon Trail

New England Seaport

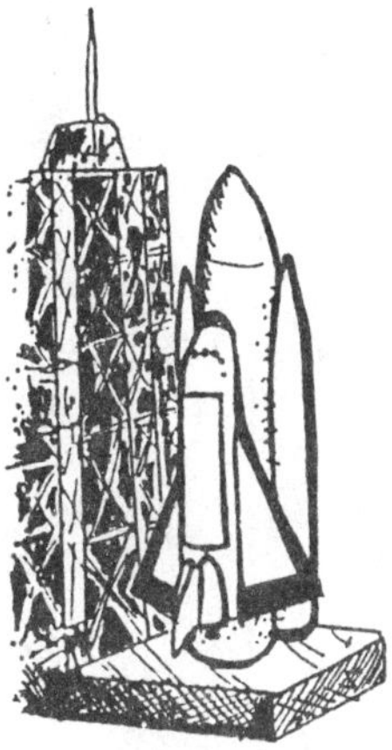

Cape Canaveral

Light House

U.S.S. *Arizona* Memorial, Pearl Harbor

Pony Express Station

Mt. McKinley

Dodge City

Golden Gate Bridge

© 1991 Teacher Created Materials, Inc.   41   #142 *Patriotic Patterns & Clip Art*

Monuments & Memorials

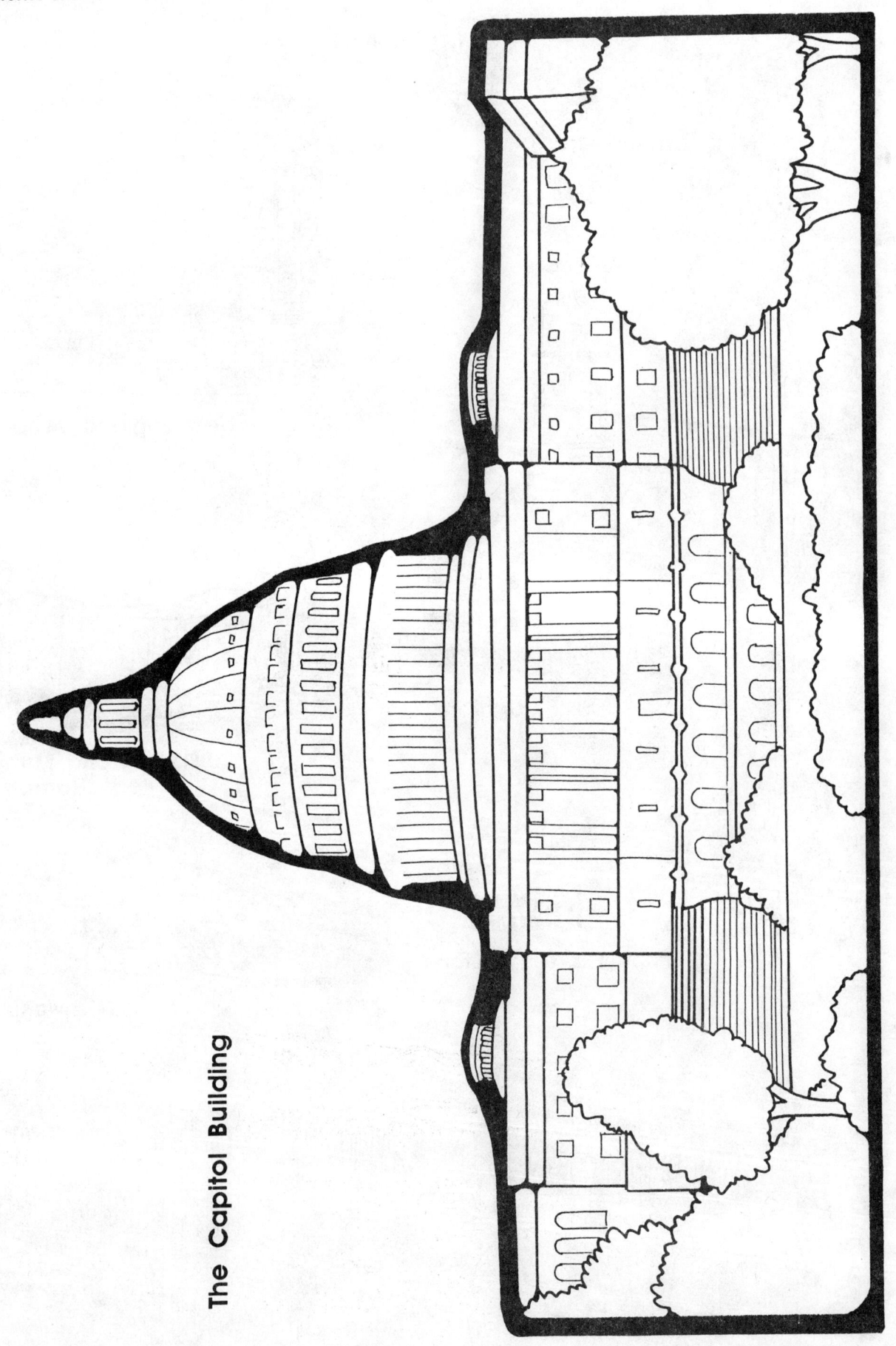

The Capitol Building

Monuments & Memorials

Liberty Enlightening the World

Independence Hall

Ellis Island Immigration Museum

© 1991 Teacher Created Materials, Inc. #142 *Patriotic Patterns & Clip Art*

Monuments & Memorials

The White House

#142 Patriotic Patterns & Clip Art   44   © 1991 Teacher Created Materials, Inc.

Monuments & Memorials

The White House

Mt. Rushmore

U.S. Capitol

© 1991 Teacher Created Materials, Inc.

#142 *Patriotic Patterns & Clip Art*

Monuments & Memorials

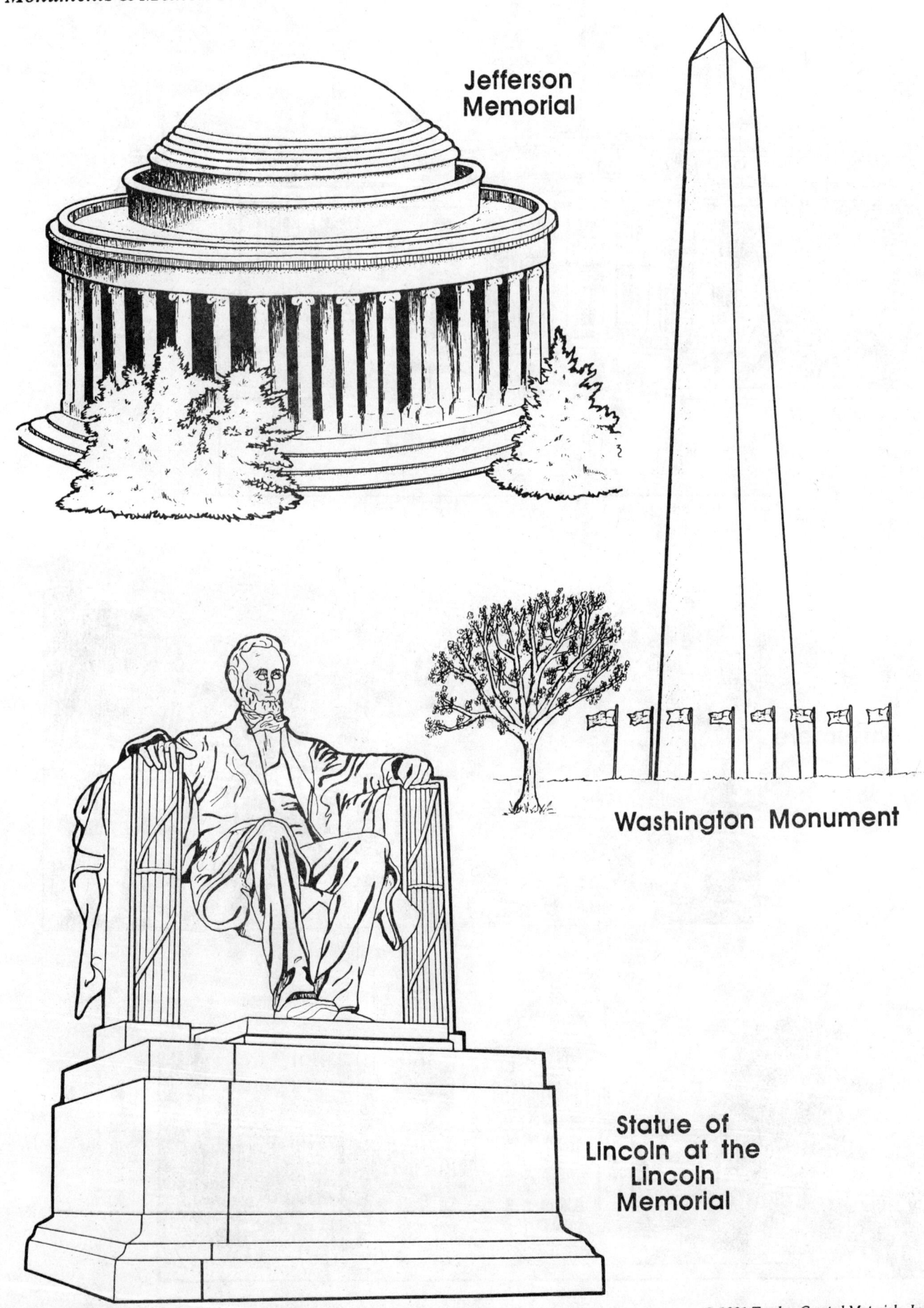

Jefferson Memorial

Washington Monument

Statue of Lincoln at the Lincoln Memorial

#142 Patriotic Patterns & Clip Art

© 1991 Teacher Created Materials, Inc.

Monuments & Memorials

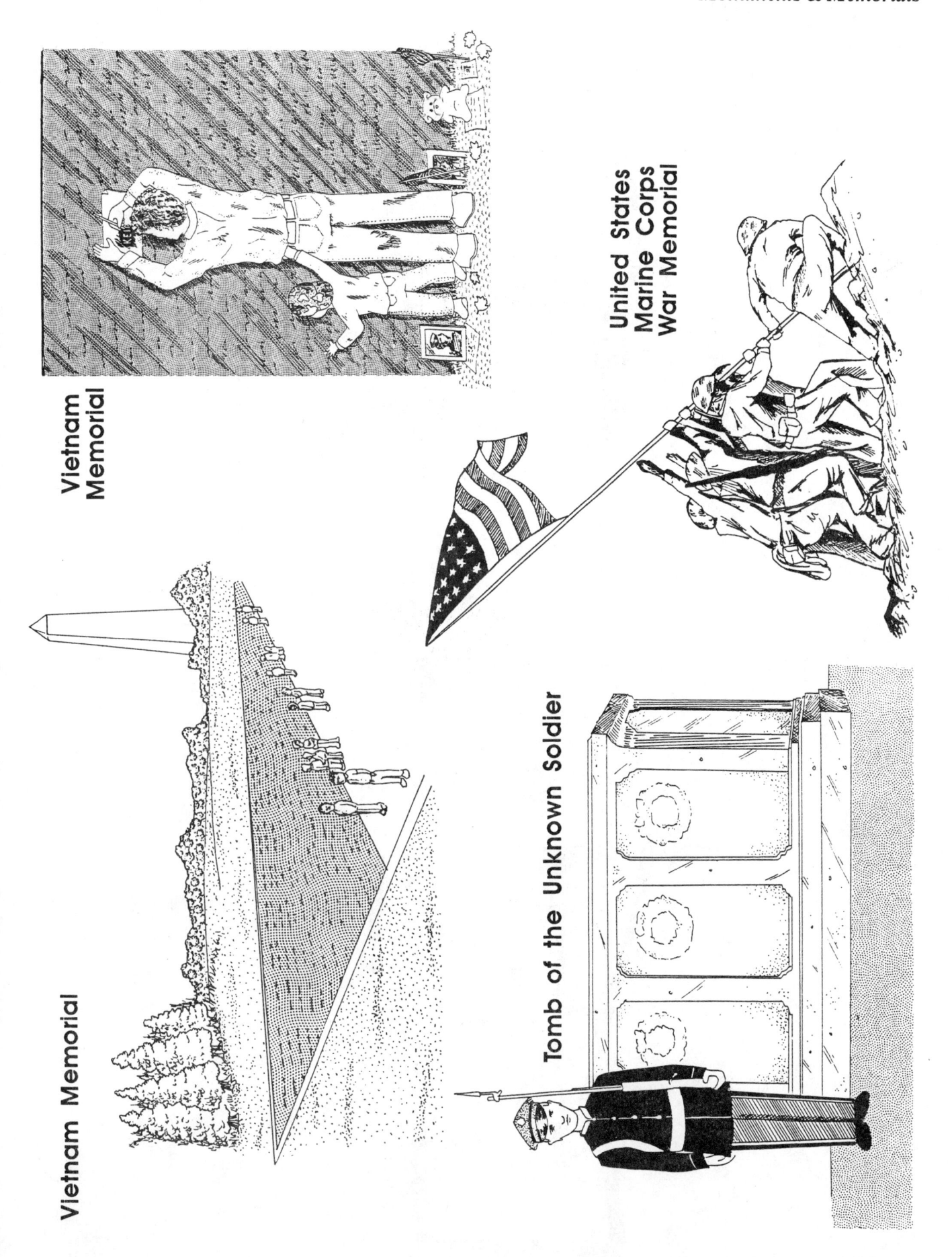

Vietnam Memorial

United States Marine Corps War Memorial

Vietnam Memorial

Tomb of the Unknown Soldier

© 1991 Teacher Created Materials, Inc.

#142 Patriotic Patterns & Clip Art

Monuments & Memorials

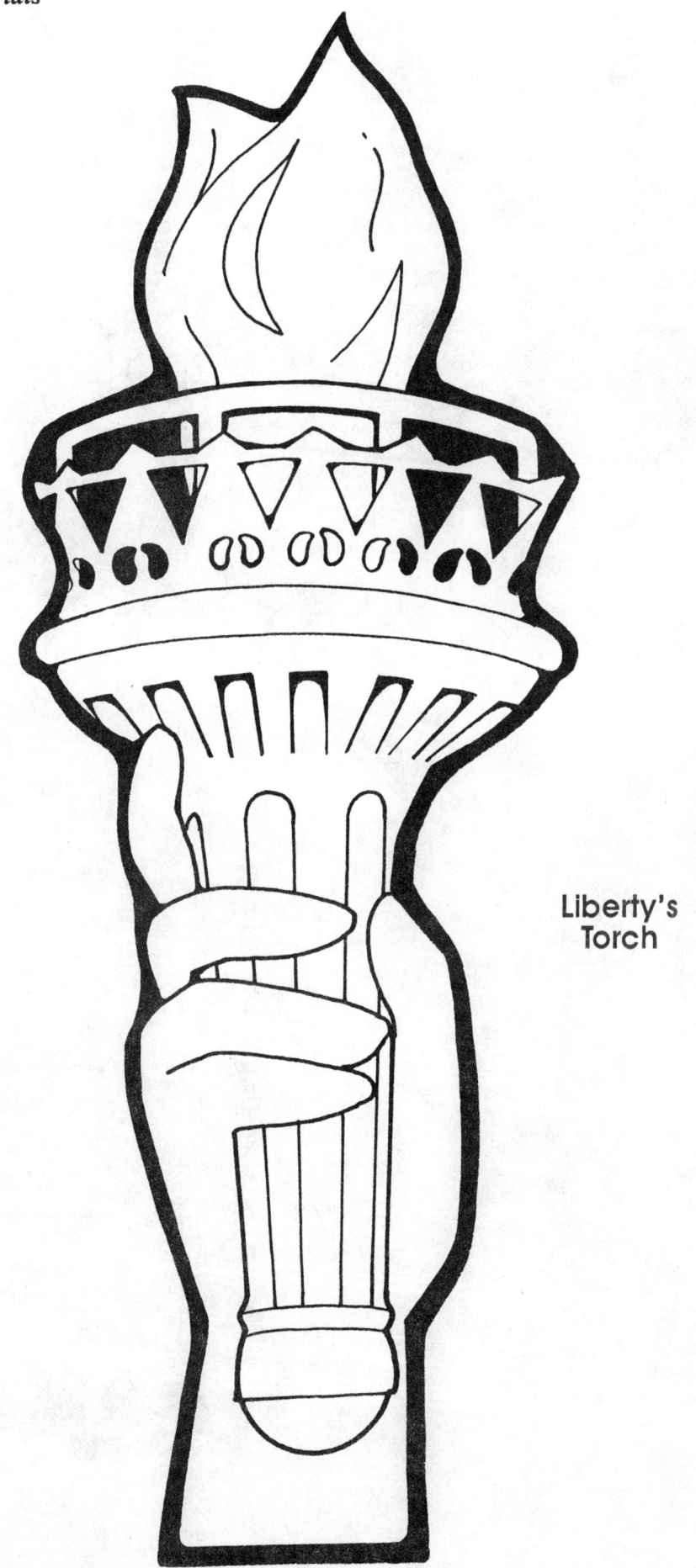

Liberty's Torch

#142 Patriotic Patterns & Clip Art 48 © 1991 Teacher Created Materials, Inc.

Patriotic Holidays – Columbus Day

© 1991 Teacher Created Materials, Inc. 49 #142 Patriotic Patterns & Clip Art

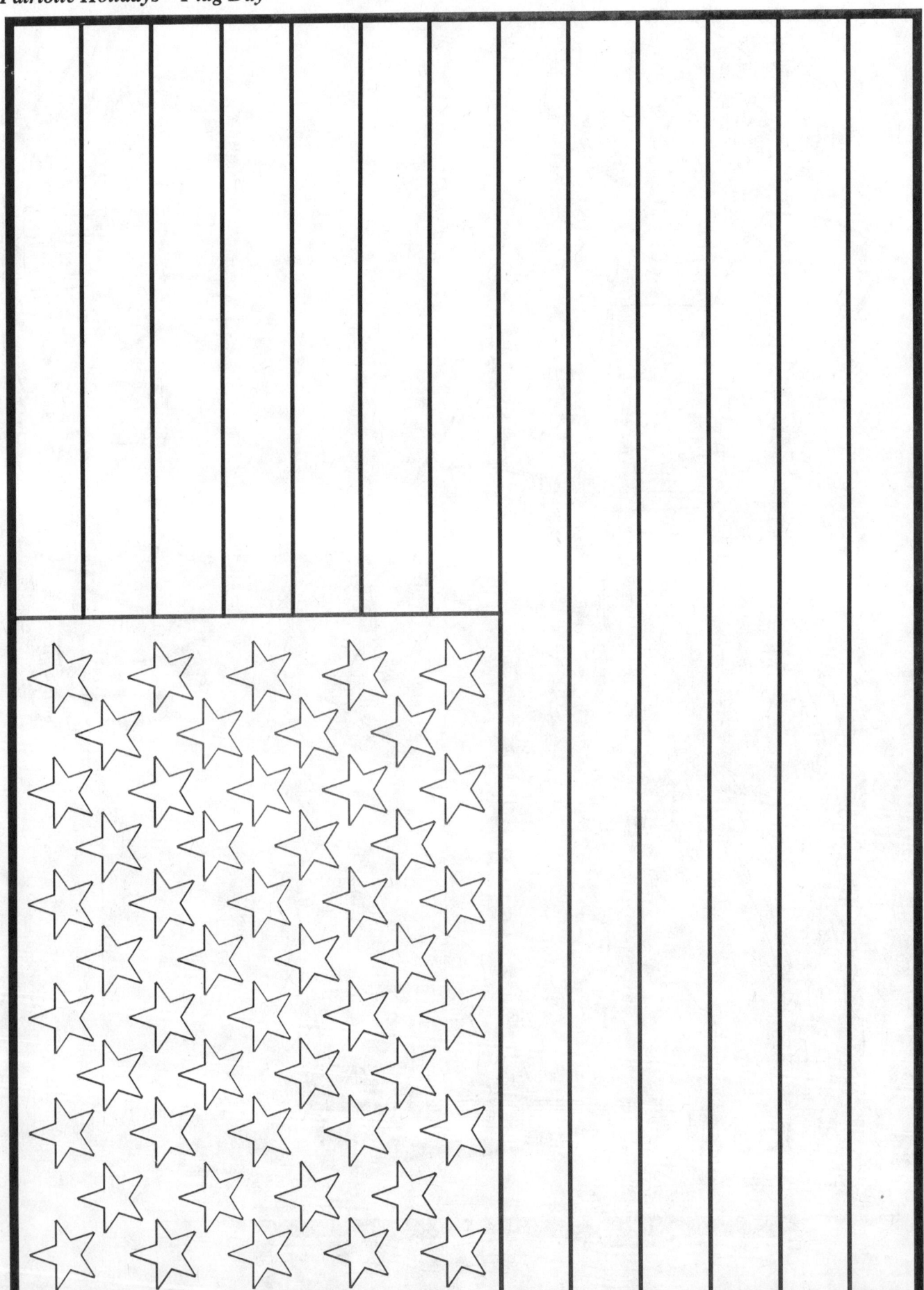

Patriotic Holidays – Flag Day

Patriotic Holidays – Flag Day

© 1991 Teacher Created Materials, Inc. #142 Patriotic Patterns & Clip Art

Patriotic Holidays – Independence Day

Patriotic Holidays – Independence Day

Happy Fourth of July!

© 1991 Teacher Created Materials, Inc. 53 #142 Patriotic Patterns & Clip Art

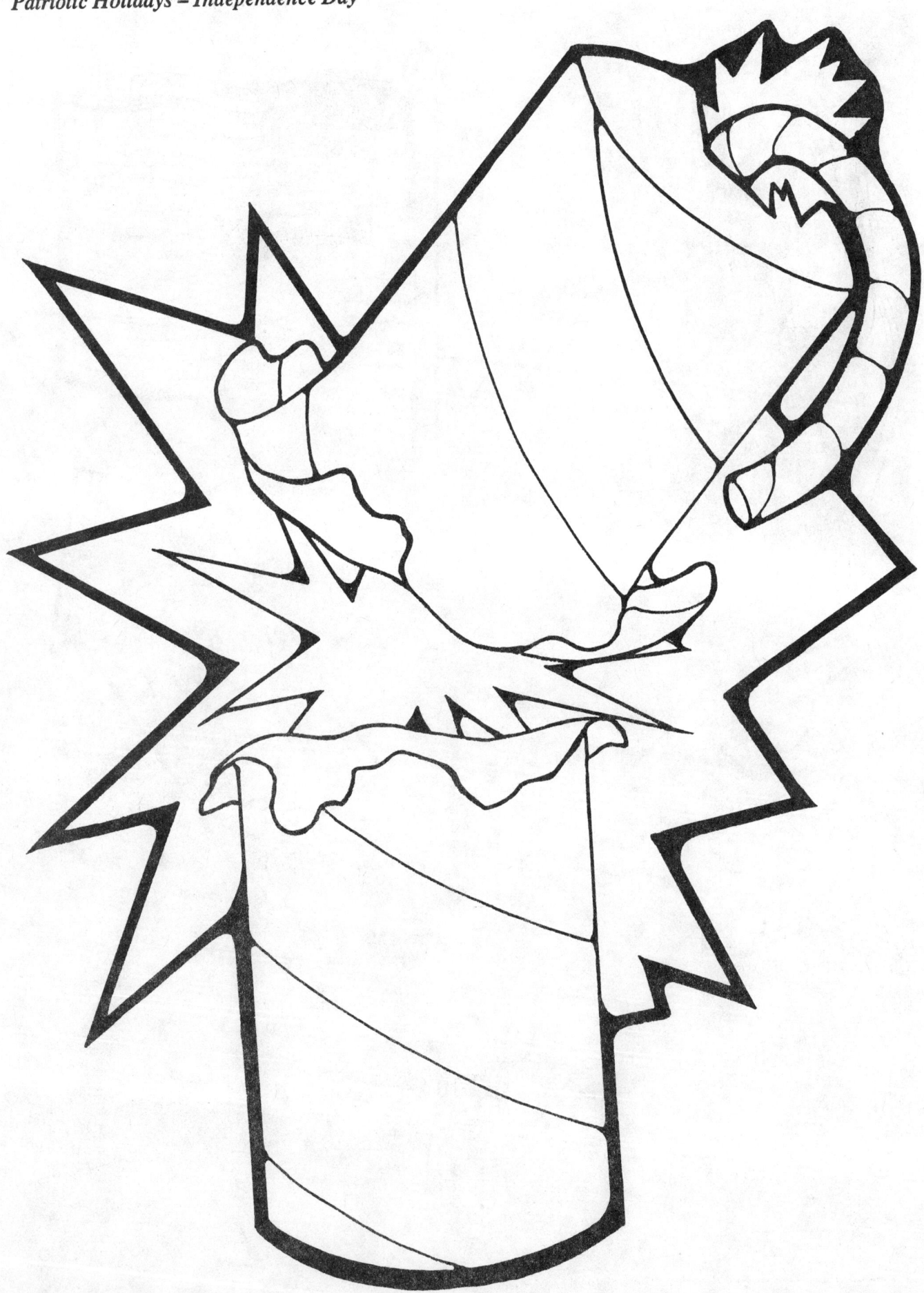

Patriotic Holidays – Independence Day

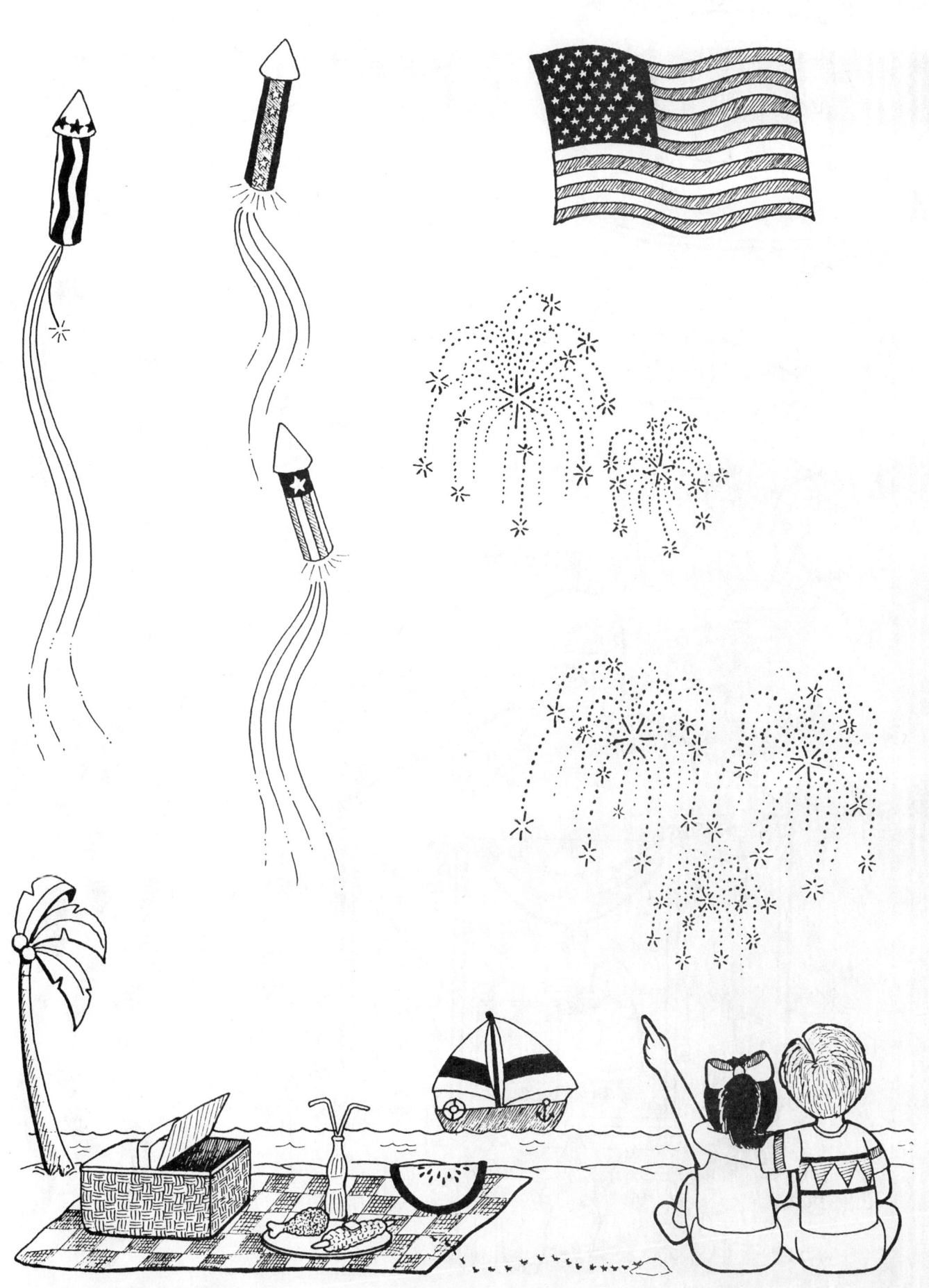

Patriotic Holidays – Independence Day

Patriotic Holidays – Independence Day

#142 Patriotic Patterns & Clip Art   56   © 1991 Teacher Created Materials, Inc.

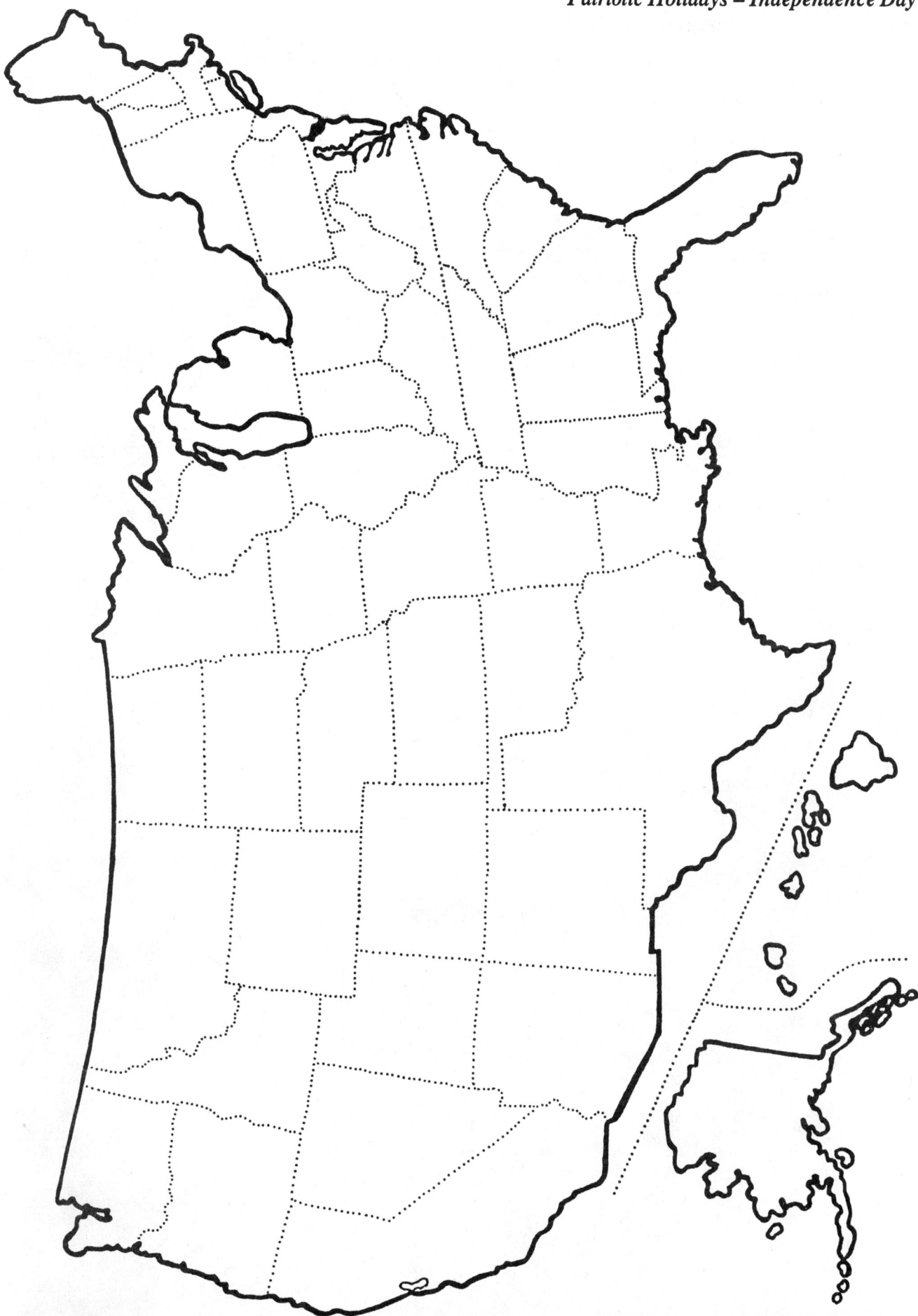

Patriotic Holidays – Independence Day

Patriotic Holidays – Martin Luther King, Jr. Day

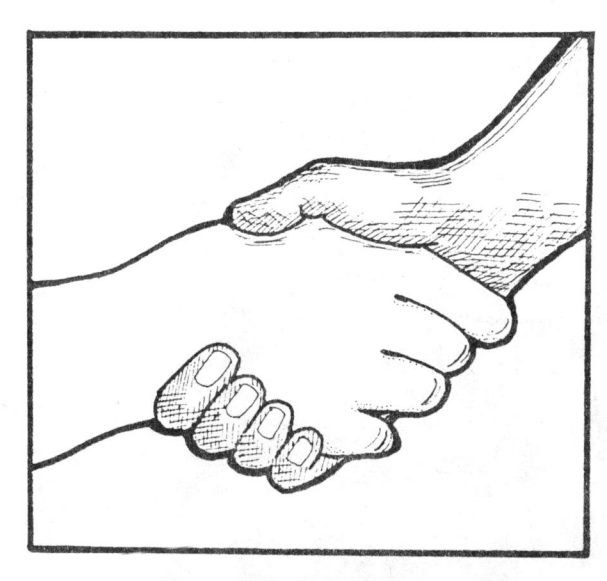

Patriotic Holidays – Martin Luther King, Jr. Day

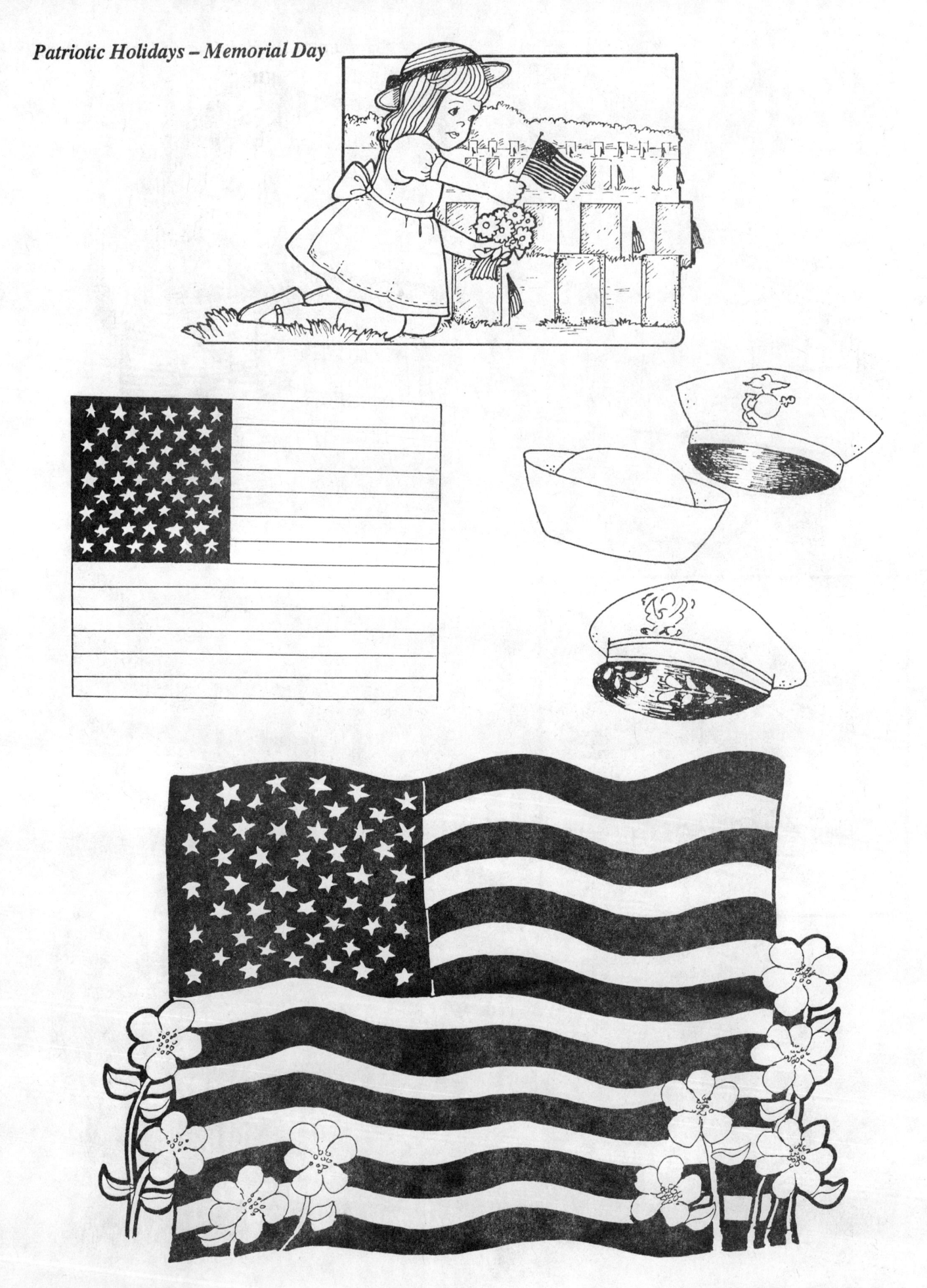

Patriotic Holidays – Memorial Day

#142 Patriotic Patterns & Clip Art

60

© 1991 Teacher Created Materials, Inc.

Patriotic Holidays – Memorial Day

Patriotic Holidays – President's Day

#142 Patriotic Patterns & Clip Art

62

© 1991 Teacher Created Materials, Inc.

Patriotic Holidays – President's Day

© 1991 Teacher Created Materials, Inc. #142 Patriotic Patterns & Clip Art

Patriotic Holidays – President's Day

#142 Patriotic Patterns & Clip Art © 1991 Teacher Created Materials, Inc.

Patriotic Holidays – President's Day

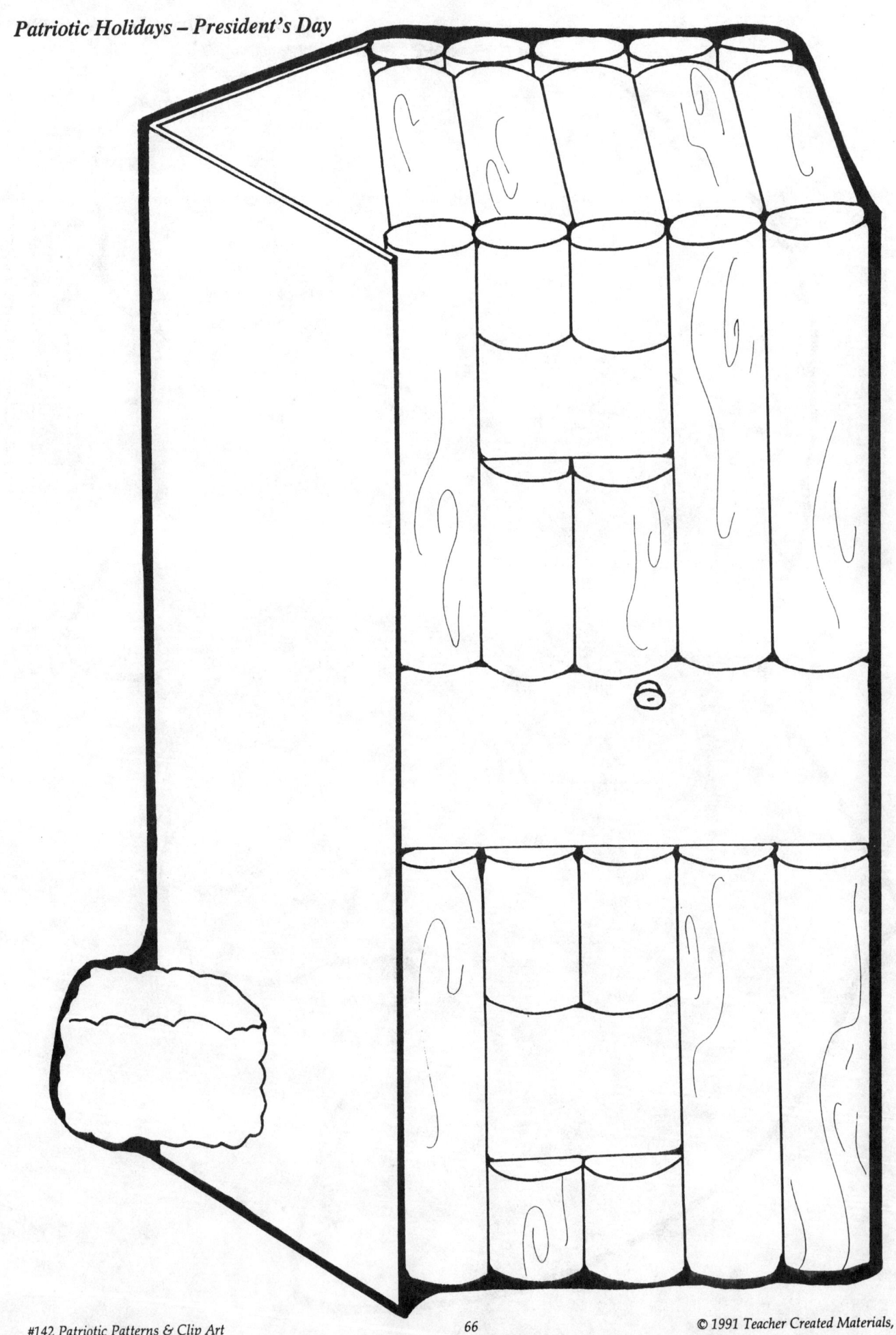

Patriotic Holidays – President's Day

#142 Patriotic Patterns & Clip Art · 66 · © 1991 Teacher Created Materials, Inc.

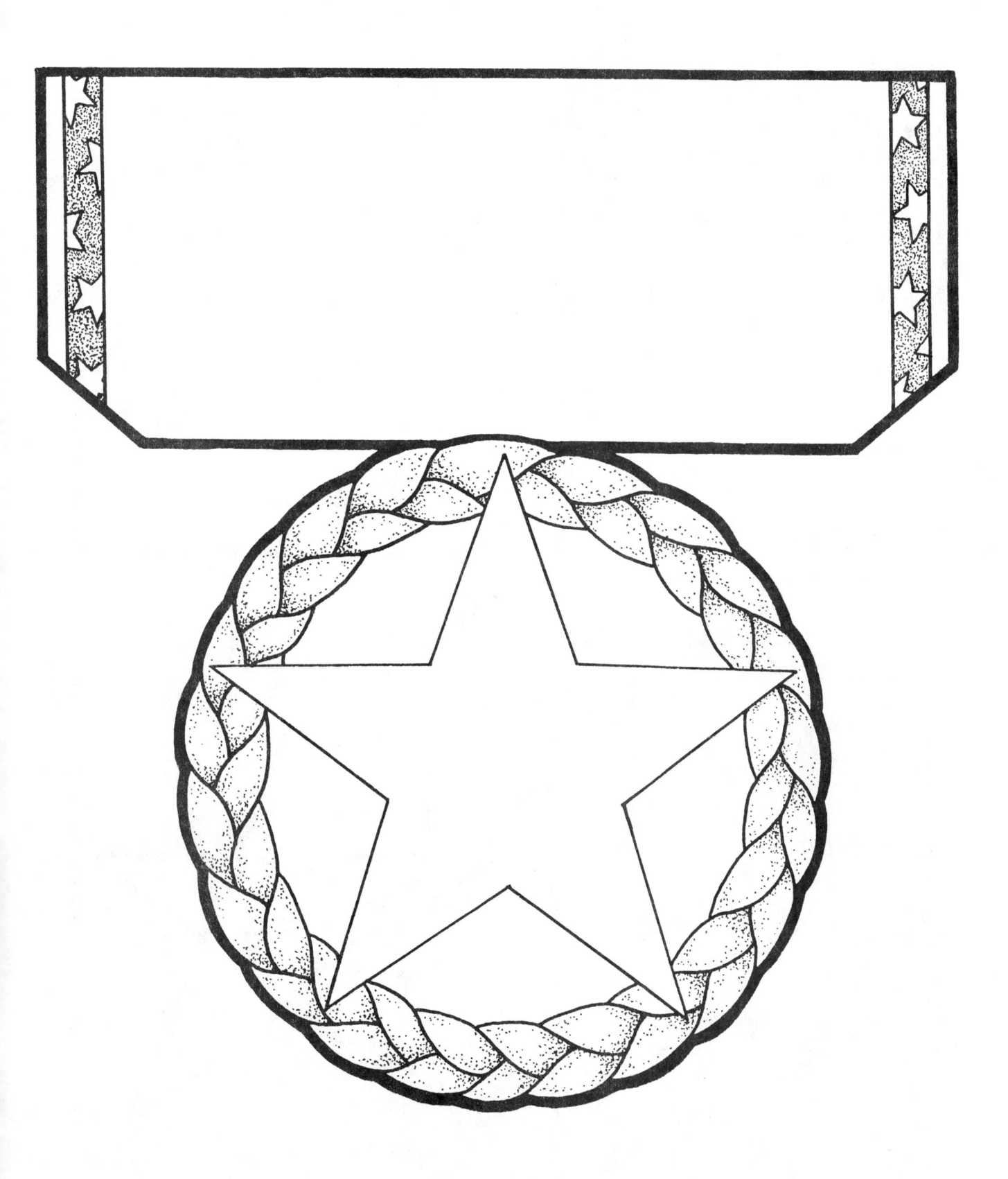

Patriotic Holidays – Veteran's Day

© 1991 Teacher Created Materials, Inc. 67 #142 Patriotic Patterns & Clip Art

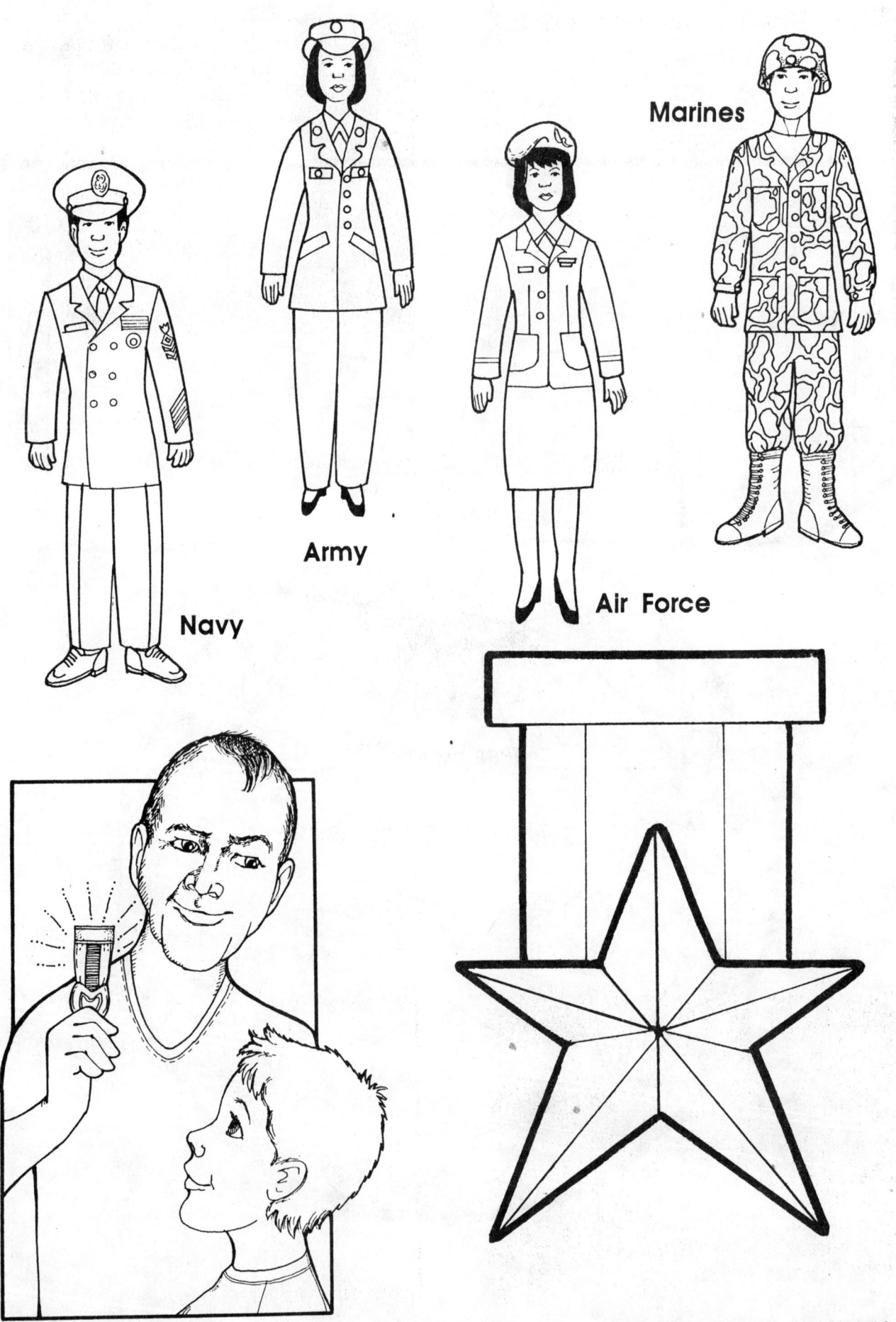

Patriotic Holidays – Veteran's Day

Navy

Army

Air Force

Marines

#142 Patriotic Patterns & Clip Art

© 1991 Teacher Created Materials, Inc.

Patriotic Holidays – Veteran's Day

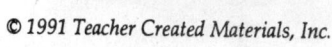

© 1991 Teacher Created Materials, Inc.

#142 Patriotic Patterns & Clip Art

People

John Hancock

Patrick Henry

Thomas Jefferson

George Washington

John Adams

Founding Fathers

#142 Patriotic Patterns & Clip Art © 1991 Teacher Created Materials, Inc.

People

Harriet Tubman

Chief Joseph

Eleanor Roosevelt

Frederick Douglass

Benjamin Franklin

People

Betsy Ross

Abraham Lincoln

Susan B. Anthony

Daniel Boone

Clara Barton

Benjamin Franklin

People

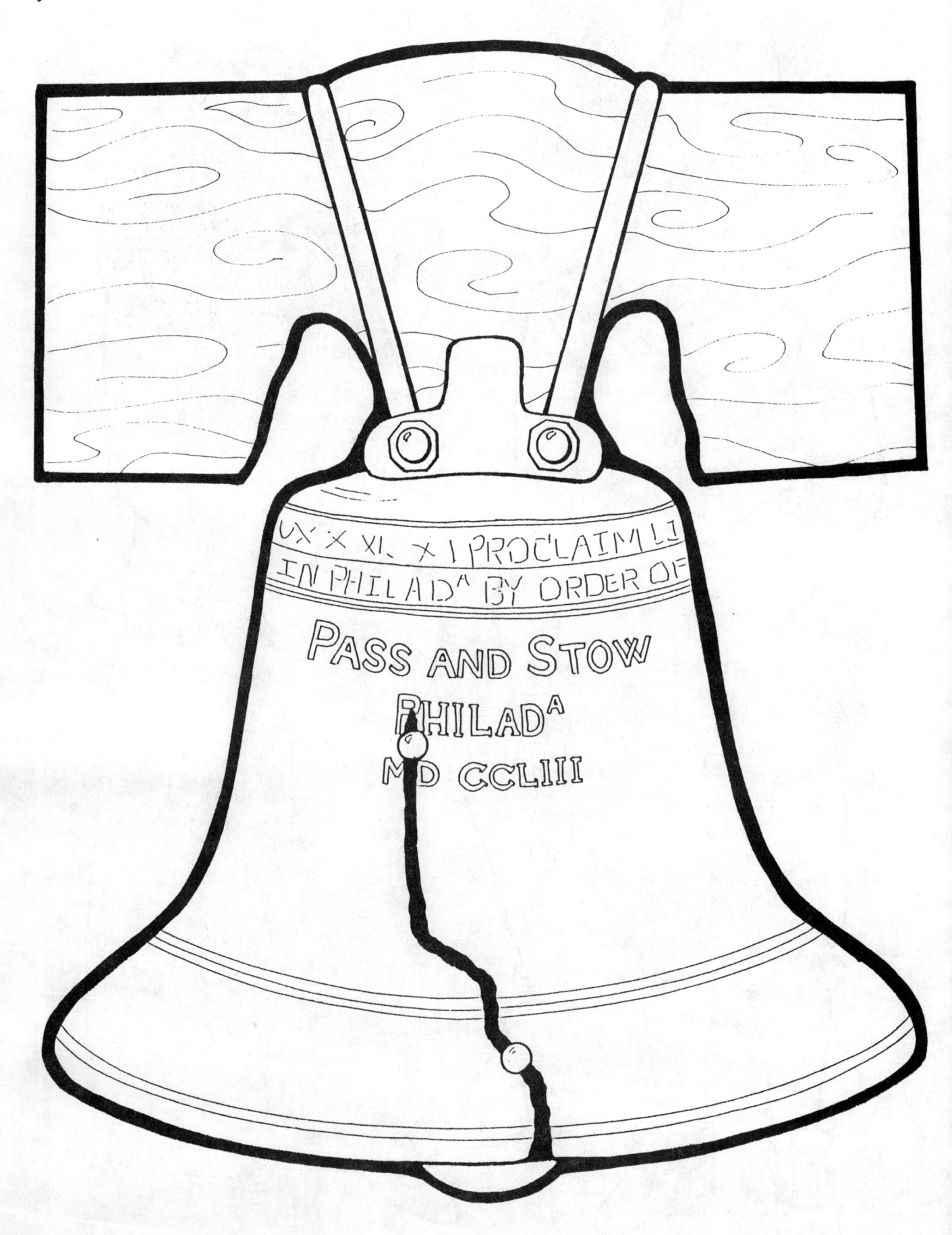

Symbols

Symbols

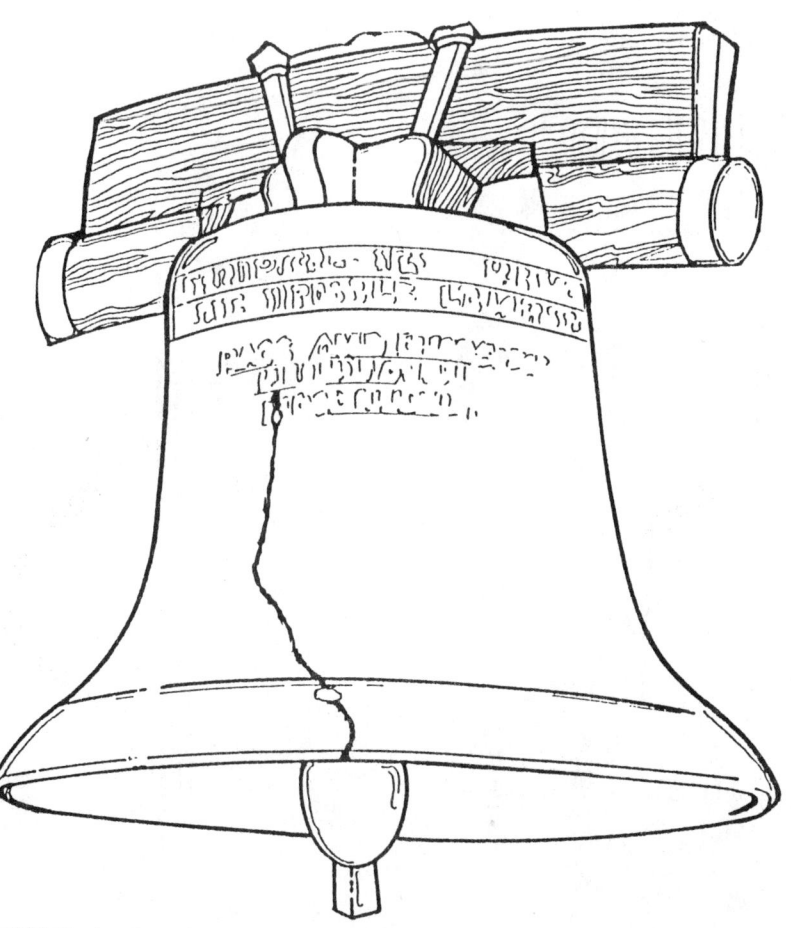

... and called
it macaroni

© 1991 Teacher Created Materials, Inc.   75   #142 Patriotic Patterns & Clip Art

Symbols

#142 Patriotic Patterns & Clip Art

76

© 1991 Teacher Created Materials, Inc.

Symbols

Symbols

#142 Patriotic Patterns & Clip Art   © 1991 Teacher Created Materials, Inc.

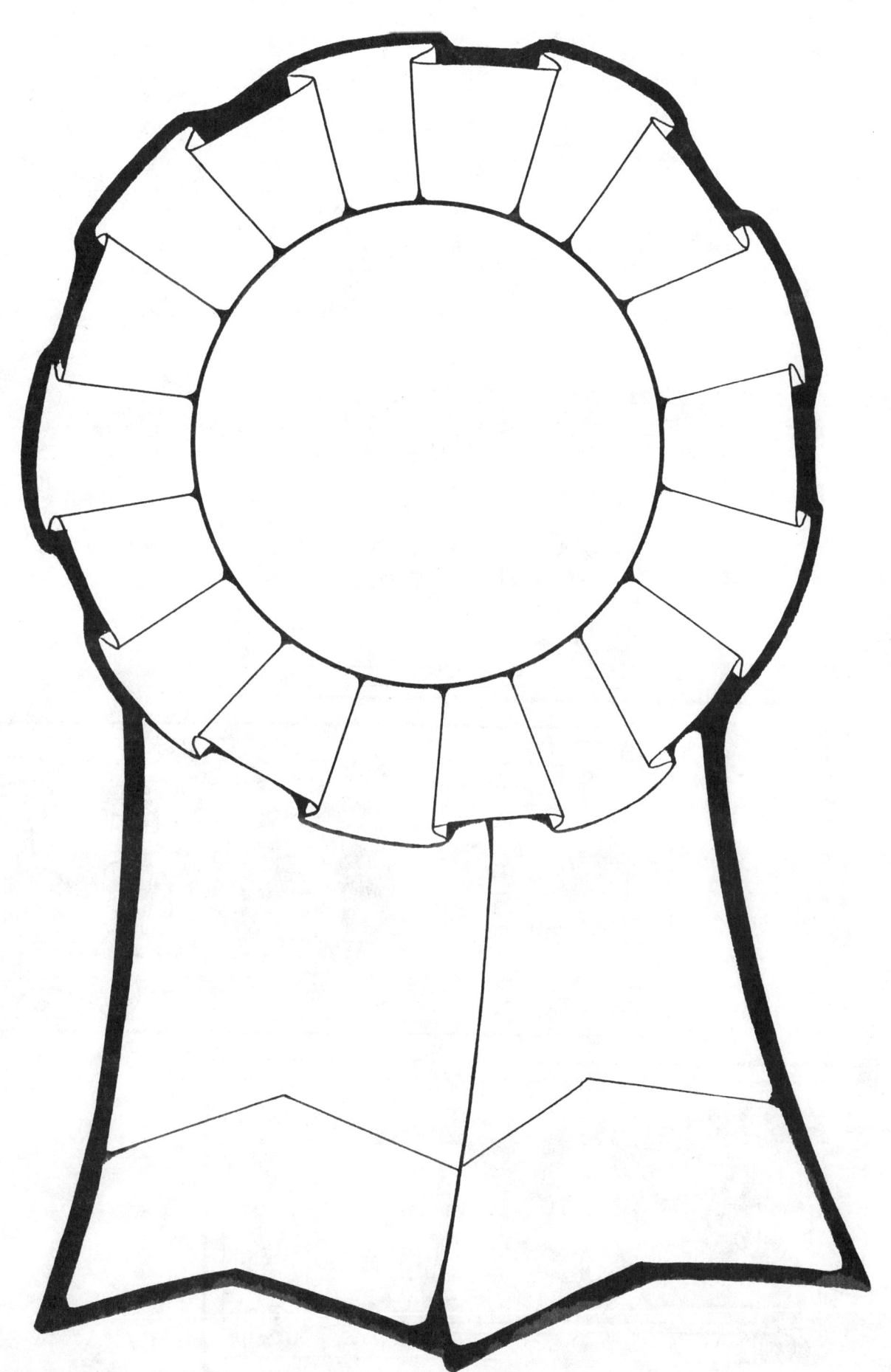

Symbols

Symbols